Dante Bonutto (*Kerrang*) -'Mama's Boys *raison d'etre* was the music, not the lifestyle. It will become the subject for connoisseurs in the future. These were musicians, not entertainers'

Biff Byford (Saxon) – 'Three brothers playing in the same band -a bit unique in rock to say the least. I thought they were a great live band: bluesy, Celtic and hard rock, all rolled into one. '

Warren de Martini (Ratt) – 'We loved this band. We didn't realize it then but this was a major peak in all our lives: the juxtaposition of dreams and reality. '

'Fast' Eddie Clarke (Motörhead & Fastway) – 'They were a talented band man, absolutely cooking. I was heavily impressed. '

Rickey Medlocke (Blackfoot & Lynyrd Skynyrd) – '[Blackfoot and Mama's Boys] shared common ground with the blues: two soulful bands very much enriched by feel. '

Toby Jepson (Little Angels & Fastway) – 'I count myself lucky to be able to call myself a Mama's Boys fan. '

Barry Devlin (Horslips) – 'We started Mama's Boys off. They liked what they saw. And if that was all we ever did, then that was a good thing. '

Andy Powell (Wishbone Ash) – 'I couldn't believe how three brothers could play together like that, let alone get on together: the frenetic energy Mama's Boys put out to win over the audiences, which they clearly did. '

Chris Tsangerides (Producer) – 'Pat was a really great musician, John was the image and 'the shape thrower' but not an egoist, and Tommy had such vibrancy for life. I had such a good laugh with them, such a good laugh. '

Don Airey (Ozzy Osbourne, Rainbow and Deep Purple) – 'Those three were quite something and it was a rare treat working with them. '

Dave Ling (*Classic Rock*) – 'I loved the fact that they came from such an un-rock 'n' roll background, it gave them a unique twist. I thought the band was going to be enormous. '

Keith Murrell (Airrace) -'Never was there a band more deserving of success. Not only because of their amazing talent, but because of their attitude toward the business, and to people, the fact that just enjoyed every minute of it, and had so much enthusiasm for everything…they really were the nice guys of rock n' roll. '

Angela Rippon (BBC) – 'The musicianship of Celtus is incredibly engaging to listen to, ethereal, without ever being unfaithful to its roots. '

Barry McGuigan (World Boxing Champion) – 'Celtus was the inimitable sound of the McManus boys. They are exceptionally talented musicians and humble down-to-earth with it, which is a very refreshing virtue these days. '

'Remember the Mama's Boys? You know shy, bashful, a total strike out with the chicks.'
Telly Savalas

Runaway Dreams

The Story of Mama's Boys and Celtus

Michael J K Walsh

with a Foreword by Don Airey

Kennedy & Boyd

Kennedy & Boyd
an imprint of
Zeticula
57 St Vincent Crescent
Glasgow
G3 8NQ
Scotland.

http://www. kennedyandboyd. co. uk
admin@kennedyandboyd. co. uk

First Published in 2011
Text Copyright © Michael J K Walsh 2011
Illustrations Copyright © Original photographers 2011

ISBN 978-1-84921-096-6

Every effort has been made to secure permission for the use of the photographs in this book. Most have come from private collections while others were published in journals, the internet, and newspapers which have no known archive. Thanks to Aida Taskinbayeva for her help in getting the images ready for reproduction.

The principal photographers whose work is reproduced are: Clive Arrowsmith, Damian McCollum, Graham Smith, Lindy and John McManus, Pat and Sallie McManus, Molly McManus, Valerie and John McManus, Alain Boucly, Marco Delavaud, Neil Cooper, Hiroyuki Yoshihama, Patricia and Caroline Hochreutner, Yasushi Yoshioka, Sophie, Catherine Walsh (Sweet Cheater) and Ray Palmer.

The author would be happy to hear from anyone whose work has been reproduced here without credit and to make amends in future reprints of *Runaway Dreams*.

This book is dedicated to the memory of Joe Roberts

Contents

Acknowledgements

It's further than you might think from Omagh to Enniskillen … when you walk it. It is worse in the middle of the night, ears still ringing from the phenomenal volume of the gig, clad only in a rain-sodden pair of jeans, a sweaty Mama's Boys T-shirt, and a dubious pair of cowboy boots -hand painted white. Who, but a drunk or a hardcore fan, would make the seemingly irrational decision to hang around after a mid-week gig, knowingly miss the only possible lift back to Enniskillen, chat to the band for an hour, help to hump all their gear out to the van, and then walk 27 miles home? (See Appendix i-iii) Add to that the fact that in the early 1980s 'The Troubles' were arguably at their worst, leading to the nagging suspicion, as the endless route-march continued through the complete blackness of the night, that something just rustled in the hedge over there. Then, as the beer wears off, as a handful of early-bird motorist swerve to avoid the unexpected apparition of a straggle of youths trudging through the back roads of Fermanagh and Tyrone, and as darkness gives way to a steely shade of miserable drizzly-grey, the agonising journey comes to an end as Enniskillen finally comes into view. Far from proclaiming 'never again' however, the exhausted youths ask 'Where is the next one?', before separating and embarking on the final leg of the trip, to bed.

The funny thing is, looking back on it, almost everyone I knew at the time did similar treks from Bundoran, Belturbet, Cavan, Derrylin, Lisnaskea, Kesh, Derrygonnelly … the list goes on. It was like a rite of passage for my generation in a county where music mattered and comforts were few and far between. Sure, it involved sacrifices, and undoubtedly many of us weren't even the right age to be in a licensed premises (then again neither was the band), but the music and the camaraderie all belonged to a form of entertainment now almost gone. So what if our gutties developed a few leaky holes, and so what if we were knackered (and partially deaf) at school for a few days to come? We had experienced something special. Even when I look back on it today as a 42 year old, I still say it was worth it. Absolutely! There are plenty of things you can put down to the folly of youth and, with rolled eyes, dismiss forever. There are also plenty of things you are glad you did when you had the chance. Seeing Mama's Boys in concert is one of those things. As a fan, and as a veteran of countless nights like the one described above, I feel well qualified to tell their story.

Of course, this book did not start in 2011 but a quarter of a century earlier in the wilds of Fermanagh where a few scruffy teenagers understood the value of what they were seeing. So let us begin the 'thank yous' back there. David Johnston and Jeremy Woods did the long walks home through the night with me in the drizzle from gig after gig, while Ian Young, Allan Webb, Mark Kilpatrick and a few others, all did their pilgrimages too, albeit on a lesser scale (ie within a sensible radius of Enniskillen). Rory Byrne, Eusty Tierney and Brian Gilmer then formed a band with me called Roisin Dubh (later, Zenith) which performed the brand new *Needle in the Groove* to a bewildered wedding crowd at the Killyhevlin Hotel in Enniskillen. Niall Mills, Rowan MacNeary and Neil 'Eugene' Doherty took it a step further by forming Sweet Cheater with me and learning other Mama's Boys songs like *Belfast City Blues* to perform live as a central part of our set … in one instance for Tommy at an empty Battle of the Bands in Irvinestown Townhall (See Appendix iv). This incited a healthy rivalry with Peter McCanny, Eusty Tierney (again), Marty Tierney and Paul Jackman who, in turn, formed a rival band called LLT (Lucifer's Left Testicle).

Paul McCanny, brother of LLT guitarist Peter, kept the profile of both bands high, introducing us on one occasion by yelling at a crowd of uninterested drinkers in The Vintage 'lock up your daughters and your domestic pets, here comes Sweet Cheater. ' We went on to deafen people with a scalp-lifting version of *In the Heat of the Night* before the owners, rather unfairly, pulled the plug to prevent the last of their punters from making for the door. Paul 'Mo' Ralph deserves a mention for being a great fan and friend of the band, and for introducing them to me in 1982. The McManus brothers remember him as one of the very few people who, when ordering dinner from their mother, politely requested 'a fuckin' feed of beans, please. ' He also took the time on his trusty Stratocaster, Fred, to show me how to play *Without You* and to dissect the seemingly impossible picking style of *Runaway Dreams*.

Joe Roberts was an unlikely fan (preferring to sit on the end of his bed and strum along to Janis Joplin or Kris Kristofferson) yet made sure that his house in Kesh could be used for crashing out after Mama's Boys gigs across the road at the Lough Erne Hotel. On a personal note I wish fate had been a lot kinder to Joe and that the image of a wind swept graveyard could be excised completely from my memory.

My father also deserves some sort of mention -in fact some sort of medal -for driving us round the country to see Mama's Boys. On one freezing night he tried to sleep in the car while the gig was on at St. Ninnidh's Hall, Derrylin, but in the end had to drive right out of the village and into a country lane to get away from the racket which was keeping him awake and rattling the windows. Bleary eyed and huddled in a sheepskin coat, he returned at 2. 00am as the hall was emptying out to start the journey back into town with a reeking son and his adolescent friends. Now that is parenting at its best.

Twenty years later the idea for writing this book emerged in a chance conversation with my wife Gül İnanç in our home in Cyprus. I then contacted Lindy McManus who was a pleasure to work with, organised for me to interview John many times, and meticulously proof read the finished manuscript. Sallie McManus was extremely supportive and cooperative from the beginning too, fitted many interviews into Pat's already busy timetable, embarked on a lengthy picture hunt for many of the images that appear in this book, and also read and re-read the finished text. To both Sallie and Lindy I offer my sincere thanks. But the book could not have happened if Pat and John McManus themselves had not both given freely of their time to recall the times and the places, and to help me recreate both the ups and the downs of their colourful careers. Thanks, guys. Unfortunately I was unable to track down Mike Wilson and Joe Wynne and this remains a source of much regret. For any misrepresentation of their part in the story, I apologise.

Keith Murrell told me 'It was an exciting creative time and a time when the people who had similar interests were really tight. It was a band generation. ' Those who belonged to that 'band generation' and who gave their time to help with this book include: Don Airey, Biff Byford, 'Fast' Eddie Clarke, Warren de Martini, Rickey Medlocke, Barry Devlin, Toby Jepson, Andy Powell, John Parr, Barry McGuigan, Angela Rippon, Phil Begley, Chris Tsangerides, Michael Deeney, Dan Axtell, Jonathan Czerwik, Damian McCollum, Keith Murrell, Steve Strange, Etienne and Catherine Keith, Derwin McFarland, Dante Bonutto, Dave Ling and John Sykes. Though I have based the narrative specifically from the McManus perspective, it is testimony to them and their music that so many other notable people wanted to contribute to the book. It has been my privilege, with help from everyone mentioned, to recreate this story and to allow myself, for a moment at least, to re-live it.

Michael Walsh
2011

Illustrations

Foreword: 'Mama's Boys and Me':

Don Airey (Deep Purple)

The first I heard of Mama's Boys was on a tour bus with Ozzy in the US in 1984, when guitarist Jakey Lee played everyone on board the eponymous first album that had come out on Jive. At that time Rock was in its big hair, big production, make-up and eyeliner phase, so the raw power and simplicity of *Mama's Boys* stopped everyone in their tracks. They were playing grunge at least 15 years before anyone else! They were also on tour in the US at that time as well and we heard great reports of the live show.

I bumped into them in London during the late 80s, and in '89 Lindy approached me to play keyboards with the band on a two week summer tour of Ireland. Intrigued I said 'yes. ' They were back to being a three-piece at this time and I was impressed with their musicianship, John's singing, and what nice people they were. It was an amazing two weeks. We rehearsed in Dublin and set off playing mainly in the south. At the gig in Tullamore I remember the joint was rocking so much there was a domino effect that saw half the audience fall over – I thought a hole had opened up in the floor. We played in Ballybunion, where people go in the sea but don't swim, just stand and talk because of the jellyfish; Killarney, Dundalk, Newcastle (in the mountains of Mourne), Dublin, Cork and a few other places out of legend. On one night off we went to a pub, set up a keyboard and played Irish Jigs till midnight with the boys on fiddle, penny whistle and bodhrán (amazing!). Halfway through the evening there was a raffle. I won first prize and was presented with two live chickens in a rather natty wooden coop.

I worked with the band again in 1992 when they had a foreign backer. It meant time rehearsing in a nuclear bunker in Buchs, Switzerland, during the day, and long earnest discussions about music and politics with Pat at night in the bar of the Hotel Hirsch, before setting off round the snow-capped peaks of Europe. At a gig in the Tyrol as we left the hotel for the gig the landlady asked me to warn everyone that the village brass band were having their Xmas party next day in the hall adjacent to our rooms. I swore her to silence, got up early, escorted the players on tiptoe to their posts, and at 10. 30 am they let rip with bass drum, cymbals and 20 brass. One by one

John, Pat and Tommy's heads popped out of their hotel rooms with looks of the most utter amazement on their faces. What a day that turned out to be!

I did one more short tour with them and then we parted company. They were a great band, but as often happened in the 80s the record company had got to them. Of the various singers they had, none, in my humble opinion, could hold a candle to John. I have played with a lot of great drummers and Tommy McManus was one of them. He had a keen edge, and a mischievous way with fills. He was also one of the nicest and funniest people I have ever known in the business, and perhaps sensing he might not be around for long, lived life to the full. I remarked one morning that the lady he'd pulled at the previous gig seemed a bit young. With a twinkle in his eye he replied 'Don, if the roof is thatched, she's ready to move into.'

Hearing the marvellous Celtus album subsequently, you could sense that it was a tribute by John, Pat (and Lindy) to their lost brother. Those three were quite something and it was a rare treat working with them.

Don Airey and Pat McManus: 'two live chickens in a rather natty wooden coop'

Introduction:

It had been another one of those nights. The final bow of the three McManus brothers had brought to an end yet another blistering set, in front of yet another packed house of waving flags and hoarse punters, who had lapped up every minute, and every decibel, of the spectacle they had just witnessed. The queues which had stretched down the freezing December street for hours before the show, had not been unusual either, demonstrating, as if proof were needed, that the fans were still there – right to the very end. Now, as the last strains of the encores faded into a faint residual hissing noise (the hallmark of a good gig), the house lights came up to illuminate a legion of steaming denim clad fans making their way out of the Fuchs Rain Halle into the cold night air of Mohlin, Switzerland. They knew, as did anyone else who had listened to the show live on the radio that evening, that the exhilarating cocktail of traditional Irish music and heavy rock was as potent and as energetic as ever it had been. What they would not have been aware of was the fact that they had just witnessed Mama's Boys' final concert. When Pat and John next took the stage at the Royal Albert Hall in London, this time under the moniker Celtus, the music had changed completely and youngest brother, Tommy, was gone.

Where it all began: 'It went from mad to ridiculous in the house.'

Big John and Valerie: 'Incredibly supportive, unbelievable parents.'

Chapter 1: A Family Tradition

Tucked in at the side of the road, and overlooking Upper Lough Erne at Knockninny (Naomh Ninneadh) in County Fermanagh, is a small, fairly typical, farmhouse. To the local it is entirely unremarkable in its appearance, to the outsider it is quite idyllic in its rural setting and humble architectural style. Nothing at all betrays the fact that from it emerged one of Ireland's most distinctive, celebrated and internationally acclaimed rock bands, Mama's Boys. Though their brand of heavy rock music was more normally associated with the midlands of England, or the great urban sprawls of Los Angeles and New York, the three McManus brothers created their unique musical identity here in this tranquil and traditional setting. Perhaps that was part of what made their sound so original and why, from the very outset, the critics, fans and other bands, saw them as a cut above the rest.

And so to understand, and appreciate fully, the music of Mama's Boys, and later Celtus, one has to look not to Sunset Strip or the steel mills of the Black Country but to a musical tradition rooted in Fermanagh, and in particular, the McManus family. Under this cottage roof, thatched until about 40 years ago, a wealth of traditional Irish music has been created, collected and taught by seven generations of the same family. It still is to this day. Anyone with a love of traditional Irish music will know the house beside the lake and the McManus family which has always lived there, and very probably the McManuses will, in return, know them too. Valerie and Big John McManus are, in addition to being the parents of Pat, John and Tommy, extremely well established and respected musicians and connoisseurs in their own right. Indeed, they are descendents of the legendary fiddle player John Gunn who, in the mid-19th century, wrote down many local tunes in the one-of-a-kind *Gunn Book*. This delicate and meticulously crafted manuscript, with the melted candle wax drips on the pages from where Gunn toiled in the half-light to record the words and notes of the fiddlers and lilters surrounding him, is certainly a rare treasure and the McManuses its worthy inheritor.

Big John was born far from Fermanagh, in New York City, on November 10th, 1925, somewhere between 65th street and Lexington Avenue and, more importantly, at the heart of the Jazz Age. When he returned to Ireland at the age of six it was to an extremely uncertain future with a disillusioned family who had cared little for the 'American dream'. With the sounds of New York still ringing in his ears though Big John brought with him an internationalism to a regional music scene in and around his new home in Derrylin. Though enamoured with the traditional music which he now set himself the task of mastering he retained a hankering for the sounds of the outside world. Before long he had come to an agreement with his first cousin who was stationed with the ATS (Auxiliary Territorial Service) 100 miles away in Bangor and who had access to a military radio. At an appointed time the radio would be played down the telephone to the local shop where Big John would be waiting to hear the tunes, memorise them, and later revamp them for performance in his fledgling band. Having perfect recall was a priceless asset in those days. Later 'an auld wireless in the window' was purchased and later still a spool to spool tape machine was used to record the odd radio programme after mass on Sundays. This knowledge of music, combined with a love of performing, led to The Starlight Dance Band through which came a veritable showcase of 'new' instruments, like the mandolin and the saxophone, to Fermanagh.

John could not resist learning the sax but it proved a disappointment as he couldn't get a decent sound out of it playing it, as he was, with the mouthpiece up-side-down. For the audience it was nevertheless quite a spectacle to see the stage filled with eight smartly dressed musicians, bringing unfamiliar harmony and rhythms into the dance halls, on these weird and wonderful instruments. The stage was cluttered with an impressive array of music stands too, even if not one member of the band could read music and had to be told to turn the pages from time to time just to make a convincing show of it. Through the band Big John met Valerie Browne who, 'shaking in my shoes', came to audition as a singer in 1952. The audition was a success and not only did she become the singer, but she married Big John in 1955. Though he was lauded 'Ireland's Slim Whitman' in the press not everyone liked, or approved of, the new music, or the lifestyle associated with it. On one occasion, Valerie recalls, a priest in Scottstown, Monaghan, got the music stopped mid-song and gathered everybody around to say the rosary – band and all. Nevertheless, the sprees continued, the dance halls, the weddings and the house to house sessions, in what amounted to something close to a full time job. Big John recalls that it was only 'the roar of the cows' that would wake them up for another day on the farm after yet another late night. Uncle Hugh's wedding, it was said, lasted for seven weeks.

When 'the mess of children' came along, all six of them, they naturally gravitated towards music too and before long were included in a travelling 'clan' of McManus musicians. While supportive, Big John and Valerie did not push the children towards music against their will. Quite the contrary, when Valerie decided that perhaps John ought to go to Dublin to study the uilleann pipes with William Clancy, and when her son expressed unhappiness at doing so, the subject got dropped. Pat, like his father before him, didn't care much for the formalities and theories of music education, and soon his violin teacher at St. Aidan's High School, Joan Wilson, realised that he was simply memorising everything she demonstrated for him instead of reading it from the page. But he persevered, as did his teacher, and the basics were drilled in. The headmaster of St. Aiden's, Brian Gallagher (a member of The Starlight Dance Band), also spotted Pat's talent and wondered would it not make more sense for him to head in the direction of formal music education and perhaps towards the Ulster Orchestra itself. Valerie's uncle was a classical violinist after all, and so it seemed perfectly possible.

Instead, Big John offered some informal guidance at home and occasionally, Pat recalls, 'he'd stick his head round the door and say "I'm not sure you got that right" ... so he just let us do it ourselves. ' In the meantime Valerie would sing the same lines over and over at the kitchen sink while a very young Pat sat in the attached living room trying to figure out the harmonies that would go with her notes. John later described Pat as a 'musicaholic' saying that through music 'he lived in a world of his own. ' Barry Devlin, bass player from Horslips, noted that from that day to this not much has changed: 'The only person who needs to like Pat's playing is Pat. If there was a crowd around, then that was fine. If not then the only person he had to please, was the person most difficult to please. ' When John also described himself as 'addicted' to music it was certainly very clear that the next generation would have little choice but to carry on the family tradition.

It was not long before others started to notice the musical family, and press reports from as early as 1969 talked of Molly and Pat (not yet a teenager) playing the violin, John working on the guitar, while Valerie tackled the piano accordion. Tommy and Siobhan hadn't quite got the hang of anything yet but were certain to do so at some point in the near future. Back on the farm, and in the wider community, the boys loved the house-to-house evenings, and John remembers 'my battle, desperately trying to stay awake, to fight the sleep. I did not want to go home. ' Pat also remembers the magic of those days saying that learning an instrument was 'purely an excuse to get staying up. ' He went on

I used to hear all these characters coming in when we'd get put to bed. I couldn't have been more than five and I'd hear the music down in the kitchen and I just longed to be down there playing. That was the motivation.

An early performance for Pat (with local priest): 'In a world of his own.'

Talking about characters like Tommy and John Jo Maguire at Kinawley, and the music they produced, he remembers 'It just did something to me, I don't know what, and I thought "I want to be part of that". ' It was at one of these evenings that Sandy McConnell gave John a bodhrán for the house to house sprees, and a little later Cathal McConnell from The Boys of the Lough lent Pat a guitar. Pat then ruined one of his father's ties making a guitar strap so that at least he looked the part even if he couldn't play a note. And so it all began. The microphone continued to dangle over the radio, hooked up to the 7" spool recorder, where the boys were ready to record anything that came along that took their interest. Then over and over again it would get played until it was note perfect. Soon results followed and early signs of recognition came with an appearance on the BBC1 show *Hobby Horse* in October 1969. Presenter Cliff Morgan declared that, although he had not set out to find a genius through the program series, he might very well have done so in Pat. This was followed by a national first prize in traditional music going to the family at the Fiddler of the Oriel Festival in Monaghan in 1970. Pat was, by this time, already the Ulster junior champion at the fiddle while John had been singled out repeatedly for his competence at the bodhrán. At the Fleadh Cheoil na eÉireann in Ardara the family cleaned up. Nine year old John became the Ulster champion on the whistle while Pat, now with the All Ireland violin title under his belt, became Ulster champion for a second time. Additionally Molly and Pat were Ulster champions for duet, and John the champion for his part in the violin and whistle category. The appearances continued for the family with young Valerie picking up second prize at the New Faces Talent Competition, distinction at the Aos Og concert at the National Stadium in Dublin, various other radio and TV appearances for John (with Matt Molloy of The Chieftans), and with performances by the newly named, and ever expanding, McManus Group. This was clearly a family in which music mattered a lot, and so John remembers, with Molly learning the fiddle, Valerie the clarinet, Tommy banging away on kitchen stools, Pat fiddling, Siobhan singing, and himself agonisingly learning the uilleann pipes, 'It went from mad to ridiculous in the house. ' Though a discordant harmony reigned within the home this was not always supported or understood by their peers, as Pat later told *Kerrang* 'Once some of the kids at the school heard I was going to be on the television playing the violin, so they got hold of me and rubbed my knuckles up and down a brick wall so that I couldn't play. '

The McManus boys all agree that if one event changed the road they were on it was going to see Celtic Rock legends Horslips in concert in the

The early idea of a band (with Michael Corbet and Paddy Kelly): 'All of a sudden our whole life changed.

late 1970s. Whatever they had been learning and performing up to this point ceased to matter after this as an entirely new world opened up to them. Today, looking back on it, John muses 'All of a sudden our whole life changed.' There, clad in outrageous clothes and sporting shoulder length hair, were new Irish icons, still true to their roots but highly original and above all else, exciting. He also remembers 'Horslips looked like a bunch of rebels and that's why we liked them as well. They didn't look nice, they looked horrible, long hair and all this sort of stuff. It was fantastic.' Musically, Pat recalls, there was also just enough recognisable Irishness about Horslips to allow him a toehold

> If it had been Led Zeppelin I had gone to see that night I would have said 'Absolutely no way, I don't relate to that.' But with Horslips I got it immediately. If they had brought Black Sabbath into Drumshanbo I'd have said 'What?'

At first a little ashamed to admit their sordid discovery, they slowly broke the news of their new found admiration to each other, and then to their parents. That done, the boys then sought some sort of parental approval and so made Valerie and Big John go to see Horslips in Belturbet where, Valerie recalls, they were bowled over by, if nothing else, the volume. She remembers thinking 'My God! What's wrong with the whole country, never mind our sons? That's wild! I'll never be normal again. It was wicked. We had to hold each other coming down the stairs.' That said, they could see the value in it and Big John recalls sitting in the car in Enniskillen, hearing the boys from St. Michael's School whistling Horslips songs as they walked home, and thinking that this at least was keeping traditional Irish music alive. Far from being the 'bastardisation' of Irish music, as John had feared his father might feel, both parents could actually see a musical connection between rock and the more traditional tunes they were used to through, in Valerie's words, 'its wildness.'

From here Pat and John started to toy with the idea of cutting loose from The McManus Group and going it alone. John was in no doubt about which instrument he wanted to master from the moment he saw the Hoffner, semi-acoustic, electric bass that his father had just bought from Paddy Clark's grocer's shop. With no idea how to tune it, however, the strings soon broke and the body caved in completely as he tried to match the tuning of a guitar. Pat took to the guitar without much difficulty, basically doing what he could to transfer his knowledge of fingering from the violin to the fret board. With sister, Molly, singing, a family friend called Nigel McKenna on

The boys by the lough: 'Like a tree with three branches.'

'They were a small mobile intelligent unit; genuine music fans.' (Barry Devlin, Horslips)

10

drums, and his cousin Roderick standing in on guitar from time to time, a new band called Decade was formed. Tommy was quite simply too young when the first of the jams started to happen in Paddy McKenna's garage and when the band actually got a gig at the Longford Arms. Valerie recalls however that he was not going to be left out of this arrangement for long and so when he was old enough to participate at all, the three brothers banded together and became, in her words, 'like a tree with three branches': irrevocably intertwined yet complimentary. Tommy's musical contribution was important in another way too, as John remembers

> We were so completely ignorant to anything outside of Irish traditional music. Tommy, being the youngest, was more inclined to listen to the radio and was a massive influence in us getting away from the fiddle and flute and picking up the electric instruments.

Pat corroborates 'Myself and John were purists in Irish traditional music. Tommy was the disco bopper.' Tommy himself told a journalist a little later that he had had his sights on much grander things from the very beginning, saying 'I could think of better things to do than sit there hitting a piece of stick off goats' skin.'

Big John and Valerie had no problem giving their blessing to the three boys and their musical ambitions, helping them to find gigs and in some cases covering their costs. They also, by way of a leg up, allowed the boys to have a little set of their own during The McManus Group concerts in the pubs and hotels where they could, in the middle of the waltzes and fox trots, insert the odd 'rock' number like *Trouble with a Capital T* by Horslips. The dance hall and hotel scene was far from glitzy, however, and was in many cases something close to soul-destroying. John remembers that, as a kid, all he had wanted on a nice sunny day was to play football, but instead he was in a smoky venue, watching drunks fighting 'in the toilets of some stinking pub over nothing' and behaving 'in such a ridiculous manner.'

> It wasn't a very nice image at all. I didn't like it. It was great when we were playing at home, or at a session at someone's house where people were listening, but when we played the weddings and pubs people came to drink and to play pool. You felt totally deflated by that. Play whatever you want to play because no-one is listening anyway. We used that as an excuse and a reason to develop ourselves.

Pat hated many of the venues too saying 'The folk audiences were the worst. If they weren't flat out drunk then they'd be turning their backs on you.

Tommy and his mum: 'We may not have him for very long.'

MIRACLE SINGER

THE Vatican is keeping a close watch on a 14-year-old Fermanagh rock singer.

Not because Schoolboy Tommy McManus and his two brothers from Derrylin near Enniskillen are bringing out an exciting new record which could be a chart topper.

But because Tommy may be a walking miracle. When he was nine years of age it was discovered he had leukaemia and doctors only gave him a few months to live.

But his distraught parents wouldn't give in to what appeared a slow and inevitable death and took him to Lourdes.

Within months puzzled doctors pronounced the young Fermanagh schoolboy cured and fit and well. Only last week more tests in Belfast's Royal Victoria Hospital showed no sign of the deadly disease.

Now the church authorities are studying the case and combing the church records in the long and tedious procedure followed before a cure can be officially declared.

In the meantime while the churchmen and doctors puzzle over the "miracle" young Tommy and his brothers Pat (21) and John (49) are keeping their fingers crossed that their new record due to be released in Dublin and Belfast on the Pussy label will be a big success.

The McManus brothers who sing under the name "Mama's Boys" started as Irish folk musicians playing with their parents in a family group on the cross border cabaret circuit.

All are experienced musicians – Pat is a former all-Ireland champion fiddler and John is a champion tin whistle player and plays the Uileann pipes.

But all that changed when young Tommy got a set of drums and started jam sessions. Before long the two older brothers were not only banging out rock music but were writing their own material.

Their first LP was released in March and contained much of their own work. The "A" side of their new single is "High Energy Weekend" and was produced by Barney Devlin of Horslips.

'Miracle Singer' The Sunday World *(November 2nd 1980).*

12

Really, we were just background music and that's why we got frustrated in the end and turned to rock. '

Before long it became clear that the younger audience members who actually were listening wanted not the parents' music but that of their boys. People would start shouting up from the dance floor 'Play something by Rory Gallagher or Black Sabbath or Deep Purple' and the three brothers would simply look at each other and shrug. Pat remembers 'In 1977 I knew nothing about rock music. I didn't know who Led Zeppelin were. It had completely passed me by.' And so out of curiosity, and then through an ever growing admiration for a world of music which was gradually opening up, a regular, nightly pilgrimage began to see Johnny Fean (Horslips guitarist), to observe how he wrote and performed, to soak it all in, then 'tear home, and try it out, at 4.00 in the morning.' The results were immediate and Pat remembers 'Within a year of us lifting up the instruments we were writing our own stuff.'

The front room of the farmhouse was now given over for the boys to practice in ... for a while. John remembers 'The day that mum decided it had to stop was when she went to a glass cupboard in the sitting room to get some of her best cups as someone was coming, and when she opened it everything fell out.' If for no other reason than to save the good china then, the brothers were shifted out of the house to a purpose built rehearsal shed, warmed by an old stove from the primary school across the road. John looks back on his parents' tolerance and wonders 'How they put up with it I don't know. We had no respect or consideration.' These truly were 'incredibly supportive, unbelievable parents' and in time 'our biggest fans without a doubt, with such an appreciation for rock, it is incredible.' When the rehearsals began, and when the wind was blowing in the right direction, they could be heard twelve miles away in Lisnaskea. The neighbours didn't really seem to mind, or at least they didn't say so and in fact, on warm summer evenings the local youth would buy a few cans of beer, go lie down by the shore of the lake and listen to how the band was coming along. It was in this shed, or 'The Shed' as it became known, that almost everything Mama's Boys ever recorded was written, adapted, refined and rehearsed.

The boys' carefree childhood however was about to take an extremely sinister turn when local G.P., Dr Ted O'Driscoll, became increasingly concerned about a lump on Tommy's neck. A biopsy followed and revealed that nine year old Tommy had cancer of the lymph gland. At first he was admitted to a local hospital but soon he was moved to the Royal Victoria Hospital in Belfast where, it was felt, he could get the most up-to-date treatment possible. Though Valerie was permitted to stay with her son for only a week, she unofficially extended her time in the ward for a full month, sleeping under his bed and getting him to hang the bed sheets right down to the floor so that no-one would see her. As more results came in, and as more therapy produced nothing however, the family had to face the heart-breaking reality that nine-year-old Tommy might actually be dying. Despair mounted as the months passed until the decline became so unrelenting that it was decided a pilgrimage to Lourdes was worth trying. What was there to lose after all? Immediately after his return doctors noted a marked upturn in his condition, a distinct recovery in strength, and an almost complete absence of the suffering associated with chemotherapy, like hair and tooth loss. Soon bewildered doctors could give the youngster the 'all clear.' *The Sunday World* ran an article reporting (mistakenly) on the 'Miracle Singer' who had been cured completely, noting that this had lead to unprecedented interest from the church and even from the Vatican itself. The story was reported as far away as Germany too in *Die Aktuelle* under the banner 'In der Wundergrotte von Lourdes wurde der kleine Tommy gesund' ('Little Tommy recovered (from illness) in the magical cave at Lourdes'). Valerie firmly believes to this day that, in addition to the Lourdes pilgrimage, her being physically present in the bedroom greatly enhanced Tommy's process of recovery as well as being an enormous source of comfort to both of them at such a frightening time. Accordingly, and in appreciation, she gave a charity concert at the Ritz Cinema in Enniskillen to raise funds for a Parent and Child Unit at the hospital. She was aware, as was everybody else, that this nightmare might return one day and so remembers saying to Big John 'We may not have him for very long.' There and then they agreed to buy him the one thing he wanted most of all, a full drum kit. If it could bring him any pleasure at all then surely it was worth it. The eldest daughter of the family, Molly, has a fading, but treasured, photograph of an elated youngster banging away on Christmas morning. Tommy himself would later tell a journalist that his new present was so much better than 'beatin' out rhythms on two sides of the chair.'

Relieved that this ghastly spectre had retreated and that Tommy was officially out of the woods, the three brothers turned their attention to rehearsing and to the possibility of lining up some gigs of their own. The definitive break from the parents' group came in 1978 at St. Michael's School in Enniskillen. Now with a 'tour manager' Morris McIlroy and 'roadie' Brian Curran, the newly named Pulse readied themselves for their first gig in a high school dance hall on a pouring Fermanagh night. When the entire

Tommy with his first drum kit: 'Better than beatin' out rhythms on two sides of the chair.'

Pulse: 'It wasn't youse we wanted.'

Pulse: Live on the ballroom circuit.

Pulse Live: John 'the shape thrower.'

Pulse Live: 'Featuring Ireland's fantastic 11-year-old Rock Drummer Tommy McManus.'

From Pulse to Mama's Boys: 'Lads you'll never make any money doing covers.'

family band turned up in the Renault 16, trailer and all, an apologetic, and drenched, pupil came out and, looking through the window of the car said 'I don't mean to offend you, Mr and Mrs McManus, but it wasn't youse we wanted. ' Big John also remembers the lads looking in 'and their faces fell. ' The three brothers were what they wanted and it is what they got.

Through a high-energy performance of *Hitch Hike* on the television programme *Opportunity Knocks*, hosted by an eye-opening Huey Green (who would say backstage 'I hate this fucking country' then go onstage and smile at everyone saying that there was nowhere quite like this on earth) came a number of major spin offs. Coming second to the Northern Swing Band from Magherafelt turned out to be no disgrace and in fact produced their future sound engineer Peter Kerr (son of the NSB's Des Kerr). Additionally, one of the adjudicators, Jimmy Smith, seeing the potential of the young three piece band, decided to become their manager and get them a regular slot as a support act at The Marina in Bundoran which paid £12 a week ... each. Despite the fact that Tommy was not yet in his teens, and that John and Pat were not much older (and certainly not old enough to be in licensed premises), they started a regular routine of gigs playing carefully learned classics by Lynyrd Skynyrd, AC/DC, Thin Lizzy, Rory Gallagher and Budgie. This was it as far as they were concerned. Success! One night, however, they were taken aside by a friend and told 'Lads you'll never make any money doing covers. ' Pat was bewildered as there had been no real vision of the future beyond this level of performance and certainly no thought of writing their own material. Intrigued by the prospect he retired to The Shed and became, in John's words, 'the main provider' of experimental material such as *Big Bad City*, *Rock n' Roll Craze*, *Down and Out* and *Right or Wrong*.

By the end of the 1970s Pulse was gaining momentum and in some places they were being billed rather grandly as 'The Stars of RTE, ITV and International TV, Featuring Ireland's fantastic 11-year-old Rock Drummer Tommy McManus. ' In Dublin too they had secured reasonably lucrative residencies at McGonagles and the Mount Merrion Sportsman's Inn, often supporting the increasingly popular Bogey Boys. At other gigs the fledgling rock stars were comically out of place, like at the Arches Dancing in Magherafelt where the poster announced the 'dynamic sound of Pulse' while simultaneously warning the punters to turn up in 'Proper Dress. ' Elsewhere the farce continued with the band being asked at one venue how many chairs they would need on the stage. But for a handful of astute observers there was something special about this trio, something that made them more than another show band destined for the dance hall circuit in Ireland. In addition to the eye catching kid drummer who was 'already showing enough class to shame some rock drummers twice his age,' one critic who had just seen a gig at the Blue Lagoon in Sligo wrote 'Personally I've never felt as excited about a guitarist's potential since my very first hearing of Gary Moore back in the Skid Row days.'

Whatever the reception on the relentless pub and hotel circuit around Ireland, the brothers could always find humour in each situation as it arose. On good nights they knew that this was a rung up on the ladder to success, while on other nights it was only another step on the road to nowhere. Pat remembers one occasion when the audience was 'so indifferent to what we were doing, Brian Curran the roadie, went out on stage with a brush while I sat in the side stage playing the guitar. Brian's out there with a brush … and no-one noticed.' At another gig at Ballina Town Hall a Roddy Doyle scenario played out when only a handful of people turned up and then stood around the walls of the venue leaving the dance floor totally empty. Empty, that is, except for one half-wit kicking a slipper up and down, avoiding imaginary tackles coming in from left and right. Pat remembers yelling at him from the stage 'Go on, kick it!' having given up all pretence at being a rock star for the night. Some months later, driving through Ballina again after a gig somewhere else, John remembers seeing the lads from U2 loading up their van having just played the same Town Hall. He pulled the van up beside them, wound down the window and asked how the show had gone, only to be told 'Shite! There was virtually no-one there, and one fucking eejit was kicking a slipper up and down the dance floor all night.'

The connection with Horslips was about to re-emerge again, this time with the boys' sisters, Valerie and Molly, cornering bass player Barry Devlin after a gig in Bundoran. Escape was not possible for Devlin until he understood fully that in a shed in County Fermanagh three brothers were getting seriously good at their instruments, but now needed a leg up to the next level. To their surprise Devlin said he would drive up to Derrylin and come to see them rehearse in a few weeks. Along the winding Fermanagh back roads however he got lost, and so when the expectant family, hanging out of the windows of the farm house, watched in horror as 'the yoke sailed past the house' and ended up on Knockninny Pier, Tommy was sent in hot pursuit on his BMX, skidding to a halt in a spray of gravel and panting 'It's back that way.' Devlin followed him back for, in his own words, 'a cup of tea, and then another cup of tea and possibly another cup of tea after that' with Big John and Valerie, before venturing out to The Shed to see what all the fuss was about. He remembers clearly what he saw: 'They were way better than anything I had seen that year in Ireland. A kind of melodic heavy rock, they were very tight, they had an empathy and professionalism, a sweetness of tone.' He went on 'It was evident that it was a family, young, good looking, they played good hard driving rock n' roll, they wrote their own material and there was something rural about them.' And whereas Devlin knew Horslips mixed rock and traditional music consciously, almost academically, the McManus boys did not. For them it was derived naturally from their roots, neither forced nor contrived. To everyone's even greater surprise Devlin then offered them the support slot on the gigantic 1979 Irish Tour, where he promised to keep an eye on them. It was an easy promise to keep

> In terms of minding them, they would have been more likely to mind us. They were the least trouble of anyone we ever worked with. They were a small mobile intelligent unit. Genuine music fans.

But Big John was never keen to see the boys leave and, like Valerie, was unable to sleep until he heard the lorry changing down through the gears and coming round the corner to park in front of the house at sunrise each morning. John recalls that his father even called the police and reported them missing on one occasion when they had stopped overnight, without telling anyone, at Molly's in Dublin. Though the boys 'were raving with him' they had seen his concern many times before 'coming home just as it was getting bright, and he'd be there, walking around in the garden.' On the nights that they simply could not get back to Fermanagh the boys would sleep in the truck, always aware that their younger brother had only recently recovered from a life-threatening illness. Valerie recalls that they were 'Always on the go. They came back at all hours of the morning. They used to lie in the back of the lorry and wee Tommy in between them to keep him warm. He was in remission at the time. They guarded him and looked after him so well.'

In time the members of Horslips became friends of the entire family and came back to the house after their gigs at 4.00 in the morning for a big breakfast and to play music beside the fire. In fact it was through Horslips that their manager Joe Wynne came to take the boys on and manage them full time. John recounts

> I remember Pat wakening me one night to tell me that Joe wanted to manage the band. I called him an idiot and told him that Joe was pulling his leg. It was one of those things I wanted to believe but couldn't.

Later John went on to give the manager his due saying 'If it wasn't for him I doubt if we would have got further than the rehearsal room at home. He treated us so well on the whole Horslips tour and without a shadow of doubt we would never ever, ever have done the things that we did had we not met him.' Pat also admits freely

Now in hindsight Joe was brilliant, absolutely fantastic, because he was ruthless. He had a hunger. All we ever wanted was to get to another country to play. Just to say you've travelled. To be fair it wouldn't have happened without Joe and I wouldn't have anyone say otherwise.

Joe Wynne: 'If it wasn't for him I doubt if we would have got further than the rehearsal room at home.'

One of Wynne's first major decisions was fairly drastic - to allow the name change from Pulse to Mama's Boys. This came about as he knew the internationally celebrated DJ Tony Prince at Radio Luxemburg and had gone, with his youthful protégés, to stay at his house in England. Tony Prince had previously received a cassette by Pulse, and on hearing musical similarities with early Led Zeppelin, had decided to endorse the band as fully as he could. He also wanted, from the beginning, to change the name to avoid the possibility of confusion with contemporary reggae maestros 'Steel Pulse.' Tony had then got in touch with Joe to find out more about them and had been told, amongst other things, the collective age of the band, leading Prince to conclude 'they sound like a bunch of Mama's Boys to me.' John remembers the name change with horror saying 'I hated, absolutely hated, it. It took a lot of getting used to.' Barry Devlin saw something clever in it though and recalls 'I thought it was a great name, Mama's Boys, it's ironic for a heavy rock band.' Manager Joe Wynne also liked 'the irony between name and brand of music.' Pat commented 'It's a crazy sort of a name. It contradicts everything. We don't want to be a Death anything, or an Angel anything or a Blood something.' (Denis McClean later presented a slightly different version of the story saying that over dinner one night the manager of Barclay James Harvest and Tony Prince came up with the name together). On a practical note, Pat, John and Tommy were also welcome to take whatever they wanted from Prince's cast off record collection for free. And so, armed to the teeth with Triumph, Rush, April Wine, Johnny Winter, Taste, Skid Row, Budgie, Terry Reid and a great many others, selected by what they looked like on the record sleeve, they set off for home.

The learning curve musically was steep now with every imaginable source being devoured by three eager brothers who were playing good, popular, rock music without having much idea about the history of it. When journalist Liam Mackey asked Pat about Bob Dylan, for example, the answer came 'I've heard of him. I know he's a big star or something like that.' Likewise, when John said that he had started listening to a bit of Jazz in the form of Acker Bilk, it was clear for all to see that whatever it was they were playing it was certainly not plagiarised from anyone else. During a rehearsal Pat unwittingly blasted out an Alice Cooper riff, and when it was recognised and identified to the guitarist as such, he responded 'Who is she?' They seemed to have missed the point too with reference to the rock n' roll lifestyle. When Declan Lynch asked about a future with cocaine and swimming pools, Pat replied, tongue in cheek, 'Well, where we live there's a loch beside us.' The reviewer finished with the conclusion that even if they were like 'aliens' to rock n' roll, they were honest enough and talented enough to catch up, then pass, everybody else. He signed off with 'Today Derrylin, tomorrow … ?' New manager Joe Wynne, protective of the boys and hungry for their success, saw less humour in the interview and told another journalist 'the idiot asked the boys how they were getting on with the sex and the drugs and the alcohol. Not a word about the music. Lucky for him I wasn't there. I would have given him sex and drugs and alcohol. ' Wynne knew also that they would have to relocate to Dublin as being from the country created an impossible hill to climb for any band, no matter how good they were. For example, at McGonagles Pulse had done three encores and still got no press coverage, while the Dublin support band, The Strougers, who had been nowhere near as original, got three pages in *Hot Press*. Wynne commented dismissively, 'You're either English or from Dublin if you want to make it. ' Flailing home to Fermanagh in the truck every night could only go on for so long.

There was also the question of recording something to sell at the gigs. An album was financially out of the question, but some sort of demo containing the original numbers that were forming the backbone of each nightly set might suffice. Accordingly, Joe Wynne got them into a studio near Slane Castle outside Dublin for a meagre four hours to get everything played once through, live. Big John ('Mama's Lover') gave the project his seal of approval, and indeed stamp of authority, by playing saxophone on Gershwin's *Summertime*, while Valerie ('Mama') and Molly both contributed backing vocals. A further two days were allocated for overdubs and general tinkering before *Mama's Boys: Official Bootleg* was released on Wynne's Pussy Records. With no money for things like cover design a rubber office stamp was made up and everyone took turns sitting and stamping each of the white sleeves one by one. Sales techniques and promotions were basic too with Molly doing the lights side stage, and selling the album before and after the shows. There is no accurate count of how many shifted in the end, but John estimates that it ran to, at the very least, 'shitloads. ' Barry Devlin remembers the *Official Bootleg* and its wider importance to the subsequent careers of many of those involved in this pioneering experiment

> I produced the bootleg. We did it as it was a good idea to get things out. Stephen Iredale from Mullangar was bunking in and out of school up and down the drain pipe and he engineered the bootleg. He was Horslips monitor engineer. He later went on to become U2's production manager producing the big shows, like 'Pop. ' The sound engineer from Horslips went on to be the sound engineer with the Rolling Stones. Horslips are an odd band in that everyone of their road crew did much better than we did.

An early festival appearance in Donegal.

The first single High Energy Weekend / Hitch Hike.

By mid-May 1980 Radio 2 had made the *Official Bootleg* Album of the Day, and this was followed by Radio Dublin, Northeast Radio (Dundalk) and Boyneside Radio (Drogheda), all of which made it Album of the Week. Dave Fanning even singled out *I'm Leaving Town* for inclusion in his current Top 10 Rock Tracks at number 7, beating Joy Division and Bob Dylan, and coming in behind the likes of The Rolling Stones and The Clash. For an album that had been recorded in three days, and on virtually no budget, the rewards were coming in thick and fast even if Pat reflected 'A lot more could have been done with it musically. It is a glorified demo.' On the back of it also came local recognition with the Longford Leader OTR Rock Award, and the confidence to release another single *Rolling On* with the fiddle drenched *Demon* on the B side. The A side was inspired by a fan from Carrick-on-Suir who had just lost his girlfriend by choosing to see Mama's Boys instead of going roller skating with her. This was the band's way of thanking him. Earlier *High Energy Weekend / Hitch-Hike (Live at the Crofton)* had been produced at New Keystone Studios by Barry Devlin again, and was described in the press as capturing 'all the blood and thunder of the boys' stage act.' If anybody had had any doubts about Tommy's drumming it was, here, removed once and for all. But it was *Belfast City Blues* and *Reach for the Top*, released as a single on the Scoff label through Spartan, which caught the attention of the BBC's Kid Jensen (leading to a session on his show) and Peter Powell. It was time, it seemed, to confront and talk about the reality of what was happening at home as well as revelling in the originality and competence of the music alone.

Fermanagh is right on the border of Northern Ireland and the Republic of Ireland with a mixed community of Protestants and Catholics. In the 1970s and 1980s the community was badly divided politically, and in the towns and villages you understood the political leanings of the population based on the colours of the flags attached to the lamp posts, or the painted combinations of the kerb stones. The back roads around the border were closed, or heavily patrolled by the army and police force searching every car and driver that wished to cross. In addition to the political turmoil, Fermanagh and its capital Enniskillen, were far from wealthy, the latter becoming a ghost town at night as centres of business and entertainment closed for security reasons. The atmosphere reached rock bottom in 1987 when it was hit by 'The Poppy Day Bomb' which killed eleven people, including Pat's old violin teacher's daughter, Marie.

Belfast City Blues was an attempt to deal with all of this. Far from political doctrine, it was a doleful observation of a depressing scene in which the inhabitants of Ulster relentlessly tried to carry on some sort of normal existence. Pat told one journalist 'In the north people are brought up to hate …. but things aren't as bad as they seem, the kids who live there just accept the troubles as a way of life,' then concluded nevertheless that the song was inspired 'by the appalling quality of life that everyone in Ulster is facing.' Neither supporting one community nor the other, and certainly not wishing to cash in on an internationally marketable subject, the words of *Belfast City Blues* start out with detached observations: 'It's a shame, such a shame / Another livelihood, gone up in flames.' The focus then tightens on individuals and the inevitability that leaving Northern Ireland is, for many, the only option: 'Some give up / Seems they've had enough of this war.' When John sings: 'I'm giving up / there's no future here for me' the sense of despair is tangible and his own course of action clear. As a parting shot there is an appeal 'No more blood / No more killing / I've got my life to live / And I can't live it here.' Defeated, the departing individual asks 'Why can't I stay / In the town that I love / In Belfast City?' Philip Bell described the lone voice as 'crying crestfallen, sick to death, sick of death' from an island where the young were forced to grow up too quickly and given much too long to consider their predicament. Another critic felt the pathos in both the lyrical lament and the carefully constructed musical composition, saying that songs like this might yet 'break down the religious barriers and meet with the approval of all but the most warped.' A regular feature of their set, and a favourite amongst Protestants and Catholics alike, one journalist wrote about how, live, the song itself declared 'Emotional warfare … on violence for one four minute spell when the troubles of the majestic city were swept a million miles away.' Mama's Boys, if anything, could bring the two communities closer together if only for a few hours. John remembers 'we always had both sides of the community come to the Ulster Hall just to enjoy themselves.' And with that very thought in mind the subject of the 'Troubles' was limited to just one song as no-one wanted to be reminded all night long of what they lived with all day long. Indeed, Mama's Boys wanted nothing to do with politics or violence and so John felt it important to reiterate 'We don't want to be involved in all that sectarian stuff, it has nothing to do with us, but unfortunately it is shoved down your throat every time you go out.' But it wasn't always that easy to opt out. Pat told Jay Williams that far from being an idealistic struggle, detached and played out in some distant city, 'The Troubles' permeated society all the way down to the farmhouse in Derrylin itself.

I'm just sick and tired of all the heartaches. I'm sick and tired of being searched in pubs and Woolworths. I don't want to get involved at all. It's changed so many things. There was a time when our house was an 'open house. ' If you played music it didn't matter what part of the world you came from, you could come into our house and play. There was plenty of food and drink, and the music would literally never stop. If you felt tired, you went to sleep, but that wouldn't stop everybody else from carrying on. But that all went when the violence started getting out of hand. People just aren't willing to go out at night, and our house is on the border so it was doubly bad.

The McManuses, like many other Fermanagh families, had their fair share of near misses too, being caught in an explosion at the Ballyconnell / Swanlinbar border crossing, witnessing a shooting near there, and risking their lives clearing milk churns off the road which were often used at the time as home made, and deadly, explosive devices. On other occasions, and returning from political dogma to a refreshingly human level, the young British soldiers, often scared or bored, turned out to be fans of Mama's Boys and would happily talk for ages in the middle of the night at the check points. Today John talks from his London home about how out of place they often felt.

It was difficult living and actually coping with what people in Northern Ireland were doing to each other in the first place. It didn't matter to us at all where you were from, or what your background was, or what your religion was or what your beliefs were.

He had always been reminded that when his own father had come back to Ireland from America with nothing, some of the first people to help him had been Protestants. Before The Troubles, in his own memory

They were our neighbours, they were our friends. We played with their kids. Everybody knew that nothing was going to get achieved out of the slaughter that was going on in Northern Ireland. It needed to get to a point where people tried to find some way of talking.

But that was the situation in the 1970s and so throughout the international life that then developed for the band, going home was met with mixed emotions: both euphoric and 'incredibly upsetting, it is not what you want it to be, a country you love with all your heart. ' Before long, once again, you would 'isolate yourself from it all and play music. ' Years later, John reflected

Early influences shine through (à la Jimmy Page): 'I didn't know who Led Zeppelin were. It had completely passed me by.'

Whenever anything would happen that was caused by the problem in Ireland you felt shit, you felt embarrassed, you felt you didn't want to open your mouth in case your accent got recognised. And you knew that the people that lived here were all nice people too.

Without a doubt *Belfast City Blues* had spoken to thousands, it had resonated through the consciousness of a disaffected youth and had offered some sense of solidarity in a world which seemed to be getting progressively more violent. Speaking in 2008 Pat remembers 'Ivor Talbot (guitarist from the Divine Comedy, and a Protestant) told me how much that record had meant to him and I was blown away: really honoured.'

The *Official Bootleg* contained plenty of up-beat moments too, all of which suggested a potential not yet fully discovered. The fiddle playing in *Demon* was a guaranteed ice breaker, or in John's words, a 'safety net', a 'backup device.' Who, not least after a few pints, could resist a knees-up to that kind of high energy mix of traditional Irish music, a Hoe Down and rock. Any would-be guitar hero trying to copy it at home soon worked out that the main guitar riff, and indeed the base line that thumped along underneath it, were complex indeed. In *Without You* there was also the kernel of a blues composition which morphed into a show case for Pat and his ever-evolving guitar wizardry. Though he dismisses the song with typical humility as 'a big long track [which] would waste plenty of time', for many of the fans this was the whole point of the night. Where else in the Ireland would you get the chance to see someone playing guitar with a violin bow *à la* Jimmy Page, hear an ear splitting racket imitating church bells and motorbikes, see the new hammering on technique woven into the fabric of the overall cacophony, and later on, experience a version of 'Close Encounters' played using the volume controls. Pat, it was now certain, was the master of his instrument and second to no-one, even after such a short apprenticeship.

But personal loss was about to rock the band when road manager Brian Curran was killed in a car accident. Then, with no time to recover from that bombshell, came the horrific news that their sister Valerie had also been involved in a serious road smash near Cavan and was fighting for her life in a nearby hospital. Though Big John and Valerie (senior) had left their daughter to the bus to go back to Dublin after a friend's wedding in Fermanagh, another friend had passed by immediately after and offered her a lift in their car instead. It was this car which crashed. Though the family managed to get to the hospital in time they could do nothing to save Valerie who died, aged 20, from her injuries. John remembers his sister

BRIAN CURRAN

Brian Curran, the eldest, played under-age football for Lisnaskea but his recent passion was wildfowling. He was a road manager with the Derrylin-based rock group "Mama's Boys" and was highly thought of by the three members of the group and their parents, Mr. and Mrs. John McManus.

The death of Brian Curran.

Silence on kidnapped Irish singer

From a Staff Reporter
Dublin

Police in the Irish Republic are still searching for Pat McManus, aged 22, the pop singer from Northern Ireland who was kidnapped in a Dublin street on Friday night.

The police said yesterday that there was no definite lead about his whereabouts. No ransom had been demanded

Mrs Valerie McManus, his mother, said she could think of no reason for the kidnapping. Pat was the quietest member of her family.

Mr McManus, from Derrylin, co Fermanagh, was in Dublin for an engagement at a dance hall off Grafton Street in the centre of the city with his group, Mama's Boys.

He and Peter Kerr, the road manager, went to their van in Duke Lane at about 10 pm on Friday.

Mr McManus was forced into a car by two men and driven off. Mr Kerr, who raised the alarm, was beaten about the head.

The police said: "We have made certain inquiries and everything we can do is being done. There is no definite lead."

'Silence on kidnapped Irish singer' The Times *(May 4th, 1981)*

'She was a great girl Valerie, and fun to be around, nothing was ever a problem, she was never down about anything, lots of laughs. Very similar to Tommy in fact. '

Her obituary mentioned her love of music, her ability to play it, and her love of animals. The newspaper reports from the funeral in Fermanagh said 'The girl's parents, her two sisters and three brothers were tragically-stricken figures in the great outpouring of grief for a young lady suddenly cut down in the flower of youth. 'Two years later the family wrote:

> Two years have passed now, darling Val
> Since last we saw your face
> But the picture of your loving smile
> Time never can erase
> You were more than just a daughter
> You were our little pal
> And no one else but God deserves
> To have our little Val

In the family scrap book, beneath her photo, 'Daddy's Girl' has been written by a shaky hand.

With little or no time to recover from that loss, a further body blow was received when Pat was abducted violently by four men in Dublin. John recalls the drama of the evening which centred around a restaurant outside McGonagles, where Peter Kerr came rushing in from the lorry shouting 'Call the police' and screaming that Pat had been kidnapped. The Guards, when they eventually turned up, caused more frustration, starting methodically about their business saying 'Now if you don't calm down we'll get nothing done. Take it from the beginning. 'John was yelling back at them 'From the beginning? Why don't you get out on the street and you'll probably get the fucking car. 'But they didn't and Pat was gone. John went back to his sister's house to wait for news, saying 'I felt so useless. Looking out over the city and saying "He's out there somewhere. He could be dead". 'Soon the *Times* in London was reporting the mystery of the kidnapped 22 year old 'singer', and speculating why he had been targeted. Tied, gagged and abandoned in a room with no heat, water or food, for two days, Pat was then bundled into a car again and dumped outside the Poor Clare Convent in Simmons Court Parade. Passers by untied him and took him to Donnybrook Garda station and from there to St. Vincent's Hospital. No clue was given as to

Success!

MAMA's Boys — the Fermanagh brothers who hit the headlines earlier this year when one of them was kidnapped from a Dublin club have been tipped as the group most likely to make the big time in 1982.

Just back in Ireland after a major British tour during which they released the single "Silence Is Out Of Fashion" they are to appear on the RTE pop programme SBB on December 29.

Mama's Boys "Official Bootleg Album" has just been re-released and distributed by Sparton Records.

On the road to success.

Loading up the van: 'A Toyota van packed to the roof and containing three cramped brothers set off for international stardom.'

34

why it had all happened except in the warning he had overheard during the scuffle which had said 'You won't play in that place anymore. ' At the time Joe Wynne impatiently brushed aside growing speculation that it had all been a publicity stunt, stating 'It's absolutely stupid and ludicrous to suggest that for a second. ' Years later however it emerged that it had been just that -an elaborate hoax which had left frantically worried people desperately waiting for news. Though they were all told the truth many years later, for those involved in the traumatic episode that night, every agonising minute had been very real indeed.

After such a turbulent and emotional year the three brothers knew that if they were to forge forward in the music industry it was time to leave Ireland altogether. The press, normally sceptical or basically indifferent, saw them off with a well-meaning shove saying 'Will Mama's Boys be our next export, following the footsteps of The Rats and U2? The boys are ready. '

Pat in action: 'I remember them trying to waltz or quickstep to Gentlemen Rogues one night and the sweat was blinding them.'

Chapter 2: A Riff Above the Rest

Rather than head, in time-honoured-fashion, to London Mama's Boys went instead to Switzerland -an odd choice for an Irish rock act vying to get onto a world stage. Pat looks back and agrees 'I know London would be the obvious choice, but then again, every band thought that. Maybe we could break into Europe this way. ' Basically, their booking agent had a contact there and realised that a nice club residency would not only be cheap, it would sound good in the press too. It seemed that Irish music journalists did not really pay much attention to home-grown talent until there was a real risk of losing it overseas.

An early advertisement for Mama's Boys: 'The pints went flyin'. Auld boys champed the side out of their pint glasses. '

KENNEDY STREET

ENTERPRISES LTD Presents

PLUS **MAMA'S BOYS** '81 TOUR

SEPTEMBER 28	READING Hexagon Theatre	£3.50, £2.75
SEPTEMBER 30	PETERBOROUGH Wirrina Stadium	£3.75
OCTOBER	1	MANCHESTER Apollo	£3.75, £3.25, £3
OCTOBER	2	LEICESTER De Montfort Hall	£3.75, £3.25
OCTOBER	4	LIVERPOOL Empire	£3.75, £3.25, £3
OCTOBER	5	DERBY Assembly Rooms	£3.75, £3.25
OCTOBER	6	BIRMINGHAM Odeon	£3.75, £3.25, £3
OCTOBER	7	SHEFFIELD City Hall	£3.75, £3.25, £3
OCTOBER	8	PRESTON Guild Hall	£3.75, £3.25, £3
OCTOBER	9	GLASGOW Apollo	£3.75, £3.25, £3
OCTOBER	10	EDINBURGH Odeon	£3.75, £3.25, £3
OCTOBER	11	NEWCASTLE City Hall	£3.75, £3.25, £3
OCTOBER	12	HULL City Hall	£3.75, £3.25, £2.75
OCTOBER	13	BRADFORD St. George's Hall	£3.75, £3.25, £3
OCTOBER	15	COVENTRY Coventry Theatre	£3.75, £3, £2.50
OCTOBER	16	HANLEY Victoria Hall	£3.75
OCTOBER	17	IPSWICH Gaumont	£3.75, £3.25, £3
OCTOBER	19	ST. ALBANS City Hall	£3.50
OCTOBER	20	ST. ALBANS City Hall	£3.50
OCTOBER	21	HAMMERSMITH Odeon	£4, £3.50, £3
OCTOBER	22	HAMMERSMITH Odeon	£4, £3.50, £3
OCTOBER	24	ST. AUSTELL Cornwall Coliseum	£3.75
OCTOBER	25	SOUTHAMPTON Gaumont	£3.75, £3.25, £3
OCTOBER	26	BRISTOL Colston Hall	£3.75, £3.25, £3
OCTOBER	27	OXFORD Oxford Theatre	£3.75, £3.25, £3
OCTOBER	29	GUILDFORD Civic Hall	£4

All concerts commence at 7.30pm, EXCEPT Hammersmith at 8pm

38   *The Hawkwind Tour 1981: 'My God what a lesson! You just had to grin and bear it, you couldn't walk off.'*

A press release was drafted accordingly claiming enthusiastically that they had already been signed up to 'one of Europe's biggest agencies, Bron. ' In reality, a Toyota van packed to the roof and containing three cramped brothers set off for international stardom, accompanied by limitless optimism and a bank balance that carried them only as far as the ferry. There, as no-one could stretch to the full fare Tommy, being the youngest and smallest, got stuck in a flight case from which muffled protests of 'Jesus Christ are we on the fuckin' boat yet?' were barely audible. A few days later when they finally did fetch up in Basel their residency turned out to be at a club called The Atlantis which was a fairly prestigious wine-bar. The food and accommodation was laid on and this lifted all financial pressures, letting the boys concentrate on winning over the crowd, which noticeably grew larger every night. There is some old hand-held film footage of one of these gigs in John McManus' collection which shows Pat delivering a blistering performance of *Summertime* through a voice box, John wearing his customary shades and playing a Fender bass, and a young Tommy beating his way through *Hitch-Hike*, much to the approval of the audience. The three brothers clearly felt at home in this Cavern-style atmosphere and, clad in denim and leather, certainly looked the part. For the neighbours though, in fact for the entire city district, it was way too loud and the management pleaded with them to turn it down. As they had never countenanced *reducing* the volume at any gig before they decided they needed to go and rehearse playing quietly. This was tackled in, of all places, a nuclear bomb shelter outside of the city which resembled the interior of a submarine with a spinning wheel to lock a blast proof door. Tension soon mounted in trying to perfect this unbearable request, especially when Tommy 'took the huff' and insisted on playing with brushes instead of sticks in protest. Trouble followed. Pat remembers

We actually cleared a bunker in Switzerland where we were rehearsing and a major row broke out and it was fisticuffs and drums flying and everything. Paul McGlue (one of the road crew) went out and told people 'Don't try to go in. The boys are having a good row. '

Back at The Shed in Fermanagh it had been a bit like that too. John remembers

The doors would burst open with Tommy legging it out and Pat legging it after him, across the road, over the ditch, and into the soaking meadow. You would see the spray of muck up Pat's back ...

Pat and the Flying V on the Hawkwind Tour: 'It was the most frightening experience we ever had.

because we were rowing about a song. And father would come out and say 'In the name of God hi! What are you doing?'

Pat, breathless, would pause to explain 'It is the music we are discussing dad.' Valerie remembers her sons fighting too saying that although they got on well generally 'they gutted each other at times.' Sometimes Tommy would come into the farmhouse kitchen and sit down, telling his mother 'I'm just taking a break from them.' Though the boys would fight about very little else, they would certainly come to blows over music. It mattered that much.

In due course the residency played itself out and the band headed back to Ireland in time to pick up the support slot on the 1981 Hawkwind Tour of the UK. Now this was the real thing! Though there had been one fleeting glimpse of the inimitable rock n' roll concert atmosphere earlier when they had been the warm up band for UFO in Belfast, this was a real tour, taking them to a different city every night. More than that, it was going to be in the company of a band they idolised.

The Hawkwind tour kicked off on September 28, 1981, at the Hexagon Theatre in Reading and finished on October 29 at the Guildford Civic Hall, after twenty six dates in legendary venues like the Manchester Apollo, Newcastle City Hall and the Hammersmith Odeon. By the end of it the brothers were more firmly convinced than ever before that they were in the right business. Between the shows however, it had been far from glamorous with the band and the crew all cooking, eating and sleeping on top of the equipment in the back of the truck, soaked through with condensation, and cadging some soup, or a slice of toast, from the Hawkwind caterers. In Ireland they had had a steady income and very few expenses as they had gone home every night and even used their father's diesel from the farm to run the truck. But over in England, with nothing coming in and plenty going out, things got tight. When Pat asked Joe Wynne where they were staying one night, Joe replied 'Do you see that hill over there, there.' Worse than that -the audiences were unexpectedly tough going too. Here in England, John recalls, they were

> Very, very, very different. It was the most frightening experience we ever had. We could not wait to get it over. The first show was at the Hexagon Theatre with Hawkwind at Reading and it holds about 3,000 people. We had no press, no music recordings, no nothing. We were totally out of place as well because they were all a bunch of hippies that were all heavy duty dope smokers. We finished our first song … silence … you could hear a pin drop. Not even 'Fuck off.'

Pat and John play 'A greased lightnin' rocker which hits you dead square below the belt'

And it got worse as the tour went on. Bristol, Preston ... it was really awful because there were some left over punks who for some bizarre reason started to come to Hawkwind shows, a lot of skin heads who would flick matches at you or cigarette butts and gobbing. And it never ever stopped. But my God what a lesson. You just had to grin and bear it, you couldn't walk off.

Pat also remembered the Hawkwind tour as being 'Very different. Shocking! Nervous is putting it mildly.' Though turning up 'cocky' at the Hexagon in Reading, they were soon alarmed by the fact that 'everyone was wearing white coats in the audience, like doctors, which was very odd.' He elaborated

I looked at John and he said 'We'll tear into it anyway, 1, 2, 3, 4 ... go.' Three minutes later, nothing. Complete and utter silence. Complete indifference. Can we go home? It destroyed us. Harvey Bainbridge came in with a bottle of champagne at the end of the last gig and said 'We're having this because you are the first band who started a tour and finished it with us.'

When the outing was over they knew, beyond any reasonable doubt, that a lot had been learned in this gruelling one month apprenticeship and that the lessons could soon be put into practice.

Back in Ireland, and now feeling more worldly wise, they hooked up with Horslips again to play the Savoy in Waterford. Immediately 'we knew we had achieved a lot. Before we'd finished the venue was wrecked, absolutely wrecked. The owner went ballistic.' A fine achievement indeed! Watching the transformation, Barry Devlin knew that Mama's Boys were well on their way now and that it would only be a matter of time until the world knew about these three brothers from Fermanagh. As his own great Irish institution folded he understood that it would be Mama's Boys who would take over from where Horslips left off. Devlin looks back today saying humbly 'We started them off. They liked what they saw. And if that was all we ever did, then that was a good thing.'

On the continued slog around every corner of Ireland other venues went remarkably un-wrecked as bewildered audiences tried to deal with the racket that the three boys were bringing to a 'social.' They may have seen themselves as well-travelled and seasoned rock stars but that cut no ice in the wilds of Galway or Cork. In fact with their newly purchased explosions and spark bombs, which would go off impressively at the start of each show,

John and childhood hero Phil Lynott at Lisdoonvarna: 'God knows what he was on because he was leaning out of the car window, standing up, waving at everybody.'

Tommy and Scott Gorham at Lisdoonvarna.

Pat remembers, 'The pints went flyin. ' Auld boys champed the side out of their pint glasses. ' He recalls a similar reaction to the pyrotechnics at another venue

There was another night a boy came up, he thought we'd exploded. We were playing someplace up in Donegal, and anyway with the big bombs going off at the start yer man comes flying up the hall with the extinguisher. You're on fire! You're on fire! He thought we had blown up.

There was an added bonus to using pyrotechnics and all the other rock star paraphernalia that had never been seen around these parts of Ireland before too. Pat remembers with a degree of satisfaction 'It was great if you got some cheeky young thing, looking at you, staring at you and giving you the finger, and you put the bomb off. He'd be gone, with his hand over his eyes, scared shitless. ' There is an old TV clip of just this kind of evening where Mama's Boys are playing a packed venue and blasting through *Reach for the Top*. For many fans, despite all that was yet to come, this was the Mama's Boys that they liked best: the din in the sweaty, smoky and boozy atmosphere of a hall somewhere in Ireland at about one in the morning. Pat recalls that this was what they had always wanted; even though Cork was not Madison Square Garden it was pretty close in their opinion.

We were living in a fantasy land. We would take all day preparing. We went looking for the promoter in Mitchelstown in Cork to open up the hall at 3. 00 to get the whole thing set up. We'd drive around looking for him and maybe he was up in the field. We'd track him down and he'd say
'What the hell do you want in at this time of the day for? Where are youse going with all that? Jaysus, we had TR Dallas here last night and there were eight in that band and they didn't need the half of that stuff. How many are in this band anyway?'
We said 'There are three' and he said
'No, that won't do at all. The people will think they've been conned. Who's that fellow over there?'
'That's the roadie', we replied.
'Well, get him up on the stage. It will look better. '
So Peter stood at the side of the stage at a desk pretending he was playing keyboards, pretending he was Jon Lord.

Sometimes playing a gruelling three gigs a day Ireland was still where the money was and where their reputation was steadily building. By the end of 1981 there was hardly a youth in Ireland who had not heard of Mama's Boys or, for that matter, seen them perform live. There was, as a result, a loyal and widespread fan base not just in the cities but throughout rural Ireland too. Soon it was to become a loyal legion internationally.

If there were any remaining sceptics with lingering doubts about this hard-fought-for rise to prominence, they were silenced when Mama's Boys were asked to play at the Lisdoonvarna Festival in July 1982, in the heady company of Jackson Browne, Clannad, UB40, Wishbone Ash, Dave Edmunds and Judie Tzuke. Joe Wynne had no doubts and told the press that the slot was not only timely but thoroughly deserved, and that his band had been the natural choice for such an event. At the festival site itself, for the wide-eyed McManus boys, one character stood out above all others: childhood hero Phil Lynott, arriving, as only a rock star of his stature could, in a black Mercedes. Pat remembers how he stole the show from the start saying 'God knows what he was on because he was leaning out of the car window, standing up, waving at everybody. ' Lynott soon located, and joined, Dave Edmunds and some of the members of The Chieftains, who were immersed in an all-day drinking binge, leading an incredulous Pat to remember 'We were amazed that some people could consume so much. There was a right free-for-all in there. ' At the other end of the spectrum entirely Jackson Browne arrived at the festival site with a rucksack on his back, fresh in from hiking across Ireland. When his set was done he took off again through the drizzle with no fanfare. In the world of musicians there were certainly some colourful, diverse and unpredictable characters. Yet far from intimidated by this pantheon of eccentric stars the youthful Tommy in particular fitted in like a natural and was found, after a prolonged absence, 'banging out tunes' with Jackson Browne and Dave Edmunds in their dressing room. On the stage too Mama's Boys' performance oozed confidence despite the dampening effects of the pouring rain and the Passchendaele-like quagmire in which the fans were standing. The television reports noted that against all odds 'It was not long before the rock n' roll music of Mama's Boys brought the festival to life. ' For an unsigned band they had handled the event like pros and the crowd had lapped up everything that they had been offered.

Soon after came the next *coup* when an elated Joe Wynne announced that Mama's Boys had been asked to open for the Rolling Stones at Slane. He brushed aside any suggestion that such gigs might, as yet, be a little ambitious, claiming 'I'd give up managing if this band couldn't blow U2 off stage. ' His euphoria was not to last for long however as Mama's Boys, without proper

Pat with Flying V, supporting Joan Jett at the Ulster Hall: 'Well, if it means that much to you, I'll hold on to it.'

Kerrang *becomes interested in Mama's Boys: 'That song of yours! If he plays it one more time in the sound check I'll kill him.'*

consultation, were replaced on the bill at the last minute by The Chieftains. This was a predictable and unimaginative decision by the festival organisers he claimed, brought about because Paddy Moloney knew Mick Jagger personally. Far from beaten, and having been home briefly to gather up, and throw out, all his Rolling Stones records, Joe organised an alternative festival of his own which was to have Mama's Boys headlining. This was played off the back of a lorry at the time and place where the audience from the Stones gig was emptying out and was, as a result, packed out. John laughs when he remembers how 'Joe just could not let himself be beaten. '

With such a belief in his band and with such bullish determination more impressive support slots soon materialised, the first of which emerged with the summer 1982 UK tour with Wishbone Ash. John remembers 'we grabbed the tour with both hands. We grew up listening to Wishbone Ash and were massive fans of theirs. ' Now they were on large stages again with them in venues like the Derby Assembly Rooms and the Hammersmith Odeon, even if it was costing them everything they had earned in Ireland to be there. Other venues were less regal and certainly more cramped to the point that in West Runton Tommy couldn't even get his drum stool onto the stage and had to sit on Wishbone Ash's drum riser to play his own kit. (Previously at a Horslips gig he had asked Joe Wynne to get the audience to take several paces back then set up his kit on the dance floor). Sleeping in the back of the van, on top of all the equipment again, was 'fucking miserable' but as John recalls 'We were just rock fans that were very lucky to get into these shows for free. ' Andy Powell from Wishbone Ash looks back on the tour today

> Of course we had no real idea of how they were struggling financially to make the dates. I think we were quite full of our own importance at that time, you know. Pat later told me that they'd even slept in a tent at some places, which I couldn't believe. We were, at that time, being quite the rock stars, reaping the rewards of all our prior hard work, trying out a new direction.

Nevertheless, Pat looks back on it saying 'I have very fond memories of the Wishbone Ash tour, probably more so than the Hawkwind tour. 'Wishbone Ash 'were really nice blokes. They were great to us. ' In return the members of Wishbone Ash could see so much of themselves in the brothers, and appreciate too that there was something special in the formula

> I couldn't believe how three brothers could play together like that, let alone get on together. The frenetic energy they put out also reminded

me of how we were in the beginning -this desire to make it, to win over the audiences, which they clearly did.

They liked the music too and soon Laurie Wisefield 'fell completely in love with [a prototype of] *Needle in the Groove*', so much so that an exasperated roadie told John a bit later 'Fuck me! That song of yours! If he plays it one more time in the sound check I'll kill him.' Andy Powell also remembers that 'Pat, with his guitar playing, naturally caught my ear and I believe he was playing a Flying V as well.' Indeed, Powell even tried to trade several of his own guitars for it, but Pat, who had only just got the guitar by a stroke of luck in the first place, decided 'Well, if it means that much to you, I'll hold on to it.' As it became so iconic within the band, the story of the white V with the rosewood fret board needs a bit more explanation.

Pat had seen a guitarist called Jimi Slevin in the band Firefly. Such was the genius of the man 'Lizzy had been sniffing around him at the time that they were having trouble with Brian Robertson,' but Slevin wasn't interested and in fact sold up and went to live in Germany. The next thing Pat remembers

> I was driving past McDonagh Piggots in Dublin one day and in the window was his guitar. I jammed on the brakes and said 'That's Jimi Slevin's Flying V. Lads, have you any money on you?' I think we had 20 punts between us. I went back to Joe. I plagued Joe saying 'I want that V.' It was 400 punts, pretty stiff . . .

Joe relented and Pat got Slevin's guitar. Now the white V became the unofficial symbol of the band, creating immediate visual associations with other users like Accept, Scorpions and Wishbone Ash themselves. He later bought another V with a maple neck from Vivian Campbell of Dio, and a Gibson Les Paul which would come out each night for the new single *Needle in the Groove*, but it was the white V that the fans wanted to see. Sadly, Pat no longer has it, nor any of the others, as

> In a moment of madness I sold it on the condition that I could buy it back when I wanted. It then went to Clontakilty where it was hanging up beside Noel Redding's bass in a music studio there before making its way to the Isle of Man.

The violin dating to 1719, famous for its outings in *Demon, Runaway Dreams* and *Freedom Fighters*, onto which he put '12 coats of car paint, and a volume control', disappeared too -given away in a radio competition.

Home again from the Wishbone Ash tour individual high points began to occur more regularly now, for example, when Joan Jett came to Ireland to promote the already soaring *I Love Rock n'Roll*, and the boys were asked to open for her. Though it was mesmerizing for them to watch an established celebrity at work, Pat also remembers 'I felt a bit sorry for her. She was very much the superstar, you know, she was on one floor and we weren't allowed access to her area.' John remembers her as 'a bit aloof' as they were given the choice of either going home, or joining the crowd, when they had finished their set. To stay in the backstage area, or even in their own dressing room, was not an option. Perhaps they took a little satisfaction therefore in observing a large part of the crowd in Belfast actually leaving before the headliners took to the stage.

Soon another, more extensive, touring opportunity opened up with a haul across Germany and France in the company of Accept who were promoting their new, and eye catching, *Balls to the Wall*. Importantly they were out on the road this time as equals of a well established outfit which had just blown away 70,000 people at the Monsters of Rock at Donington. John admired how 'incredibly disciplined' Accept were musically, even if they left a bit to be desired in terms of camaraderie. He recalls that in these early days the singer, Udo Dirkschneider, 'never spoke. They kept themselves to themselves. Accept were one of those bands you kept your distance from. If they spoke to you, you spoke to them, but that was it.' The bass player Peter Baltes however 'was really good fun' and a victim of their pranks. On one occasion, Pat recalls

We managed to get his bed out of the top of the Hilton Hotel, onto the roof, with him in it and left him there for the night. Peter woke up the next morning anyway and near shit himself.

Gradually, as Mama's Boys had just been signed to Virgin in France, and after especially successful shows in Lyon and Montpellier, the McManus brothers won the reciprocal respect of Accept and, in time, actually convinced the Germans to bring the band to Belfast. Pat laughs as he remembers what happened next

I do remember telling them to come to Belfast and of course they were dead scared. I convinced them that they would be really popular there, which they were, and said 'Don't worry nothing will happen to you.' So they arrived in Belfast and when they came out of the hotel the next morning the bus was burned ... They told us 'You said come

Fooling around: 'Move over Mötley Crüe and make way for Mama's Boys.'

to Ireland, and now look what has happened! Our fucking bus is burned. That's the welcome we get. '

When the European trek finished it was clear that France in particular had been absolutely won over. As such they were even advised to turn down the opening slot for Gary Moore there as they were established headliners now and a support act to no-one. Not even Gary Moore.

But it was going to take a break-through recording to get Mama's Boys established on a wider European scale. Joe Wynne asked Barry Devlin to produce a record with Philip Begley as engineer, and loosed up a budget of about £1, 500 for the job. Devlin then secured Lombard Studios in Dublin for a full week. As they had done with the *Official Bootleg* the boys simply played through everything live then used whatever time was left for 'polishing.' Begley remembers hitting it off with Pat in particular, saying that 'both of us were reading from the same hymn sheet', and with Barry Devlin completing the working trio, produced exactly the sound that was needed. Compared to the tinny sounding *Bootleg,* this came across as the real thing from the kick start of *In the Heat of the Night,* through the snarling guitars in *Silence is out of Fashion,* the thumping base in *Reach for the Top,* to the fading solo of a revamped *Belfast City Blues.*

The critical dividends were not long in coming either. Early reviews of *Plug it in* suggested that this album was something special and absolutely certain to put the boys on the map. In fact in an article called 'Socket to me!' one critic jumped the gun and, already assuming the permanence of the band and the significance of their contribution to modern Irish culture, wrote 'When, many years from now, a venerable, grey bearded Bill Graham sits down to write his Definitive History of Irish Rock in the Twentieth Century, I'd be willing to lay odds that he'll be making more than a passing reference to Mama's Boys. '

What set them aside from any number of other young bands was the fact that they were so clearly not run-of-the mill New Wave of British Heavy Metal – their music was far more important than that. One critic tried to fathom the limits of their potential suggesting 'Having conquered the metal muse perhaps they now intend to push on to pastures new', while another waxed lyrical saying 'The real triumph for Mama's Boys [...] is not just the undoubted mastery it displays them as having over the metal idiom, but in the promise it holds for their future development. ' In other words, if this is what has been achieved so far, and in such a short time, then what is next?

Of course in some places their musical naiveté shone through, and in isolated cases it came pretty close to plagiarism, but everyone agreed that it was done with such competence (and sincerity) that it could not really be criticised too harshly. *In the Heat of the Night* was seen to borrow from the legendary Robertson / Gorham guitar harmonies, *Belfast City Blues* boasted a solo like Johnny Fean's (Horslips) on *I'll be Waiting*, *Straight Forward* had more than a hint of Saxon's *Wheels of Steel* and Ted Nugent himself could have played *Burnin' Up*. That said, to this lexicon of metal / hard rock references was added an entirely original combination of 'finger-lickin', foot stamping fiddle-flurry' in *Runaway Dreams*, the 100 m. p. h. rifferama of *Reach for the Top* ('a greased lightnin' rocker which hits you dead square below the belt'), and the sheer originality and 'sleazy, swing bop' of *Needle in the Groove*. With all of this combined, Geoff Banks summed the opus up as 'a melting pot of classic heavy rock with their own distinctive style bubbling away at the top.' *Noise* recognised the record as 'Teeming with fresh ideas and new angle approaches to basic HM'; *Sounds* described it as 'a riff above the rest'; while *Kerrang* concluded that the LP was 'Choc full of winners … infected by the modern mode of metal' before announcing 'Move over Mötley Crüe and make way for Mama's Boys.'

Demon live in Derrylin: 'Finger-lickin', foot stamping, fiddle-flurry.'

Music alone was doing the talking, not all the hype and scandal generated by the Los Angeles rockers and their erstwhile followers. Philip Bell concluded with absolute confidence 'They have not been injected, infected or affected', observing instead that they cared nothing for money and stardom, but only wanted to travel and be respected as musicians. Accordingly he signed off with 'this troupe are a sure fire shot to the top.' Ironically, at the very time the band was being praised for its originality and its ethnic slant on rock n'roll, Pat maintained that they weren't aiming for that at all. He remembers with some frustration that it was odd for him to hear people saying 'You have a great Irish sound', then added 'We couldn't hear it, we thought it was an insult. We were doing our best to sound like we came from Birmingham and the Black Country.' Anyway, not burdened with a message or a war cry of any description, the boys were simply endeavouring to bring good music, with a hard edge, to the public at the rate of about 26 performances a month.

To get airplay, and so to get into the bigger venues in Ireland, and perhaps across the water to England again, a hit single was now needed and this came in the form of *Needle in the Groove*, which John remembers as a 'wicked little song, with a hypnotic riff and lyrically [it was] a bit naughty.' Pat remembers the origins of the composition: 'I was in the swing of things then' and inauspiciously 'messing about with that riff' in the studio. He had also been doodling with the idea in sound checks for quite a while to get people's reactions, but no-one had really noticed or said anything. Then 'Joe just happened to walk in when I was messing' and asked what the riff was or where it had come from. Pat replied 'Ah its nothing, I'm just tuning up.' But Joe wouldn't let it go and said 'Well it sounds good to me, put a song to that.' Pat remembers getting the whole thing straightened out in his head as they drove home in the lorry to Derrylin.

> The next day we set the gear up and 15 minutes later it was done. I don't know where the idea came from really. Maybe from hoaking around with a Steely Dan progression. Then we went back and recorded it. It only took a couple of days.

Philip Begley suggested the 'rusty megaphone' sound which got the record singled out for heavy radio play and immediately Barry Devlin, who produced the single, knew that it was a winner. In retrospect, he remarked 'It is the best ZZ Top single there never was. ZZ Top were about to turn that currency into absolute gold.' The critics, when they got hold of it, agreed and enthused about a 'firm, sleazy, swing-bop blues tune', leading

Three brothers: 'They have not been injected, infected or affected.'

Neil Jeffries, in the hallowed pages of *Kerrang*, to conclude 'The if-this-band-don't-make-it-I'll-eat-my-hat cliché is completely justified; stuff like this ought to be available on the National Health. Superb!' Dave Ling joined the ranks, talking of the 'stupendous, vibrant riff' which simply had to become a classic. Another hurdle had been overcome with increasingly predictable ease.

But to understand what the excitement was really all about, and to appreciate fully the enormity of what was unfolding, Mama's Boys had to be seen live. Accordingly, and in response to the first stirrings in the UK music press, a few journalists started making plans to see Mama's Boys on their own turf. Philip Bell tipped off Geoff Banks from *Kerrang*, tantalisingly declaring that Pat ('The Professor') had the potential to blow away Michael Schenker. Perhaps he already had. The result was immediate and Banks 'was on a plane to Ireland before you could say "Two pints of Guinness and a packet of crisps please". ' The stories that came back about the week on the road bubbled over with enthusiasm. Tommy ('The Fanny') it was reported, was the joker and the very talented sticksman who, in *Reach for the Top*, resembled Animal out of the Muppets; Pat was a prodigy with a total lack of rock star attitude who sited Bert Weedon as a major influence ('If we were looking for screaming guitars -Bert was the guy. '); and John injected nothing short of 110% star-studded charisma into every sweat soaked performance from behind a trade-mark pair of mirror shades while gunning the audience down with a well aimed bass. Each of the brothers had his own distinctive personality and musical talent to bring to the overall mêlée, making it inimitable. Tommy in particular, it was reported, 'had more energy than a barrel load of monkeys and is just about as mischievous!' (elsewhere he was described as 'the outrageous band mad child'), while the other two were described as 'workaholics' who were finally about to receive the first class education they needed and deserved. The article concluded 'With determination and talent as powerful as theirs, it's hard to imagine how they could fail. ' Banks signed off with some excitement telling the readers of the only worthwhile rock magazine in circulation at the time 'So be warned – the Irish invasion is imminent, and it won't be a day too soon. '

The TV appearances followed too, though it was hard for a talented live band to take these three minute, mimed, performances seriously. Where, traditionally, show bands dressed in white suits and even had step routines and movements to follow during their performances, Mama's Boys splashed each other with water in the toilets and then dressed down about as far as they could go. John remembers 'some of the clothes we wore were ridiculous',

Mama's Boys at the Marquee: 'So be warned – the Irish invasion is imminent, and it won't be a day too soon.'

Mama's Boys with Phil Lynott on the Thunder and Lightning Tour: 'We were like "Yes, Mr Lynott, No, Mr Lynott".'

like Pat's gorilla suit during the recording of *Runaway Dreams* at the RTE studios, or his leopard skin top and spray on trousers during the filming of *Silence is out of Fashion*. Tommy couldn't take it seriously either and on one programme totally duffed the ending of *Silence is out of Fashion* by being way out of time with the backing tape. Even at the concerts Tommy didn't allow himself to take things (or himself) too seriously and was far happier having a laugh than trying to work on some sultry rock star ego. John remembers that 'Tommy was absolutely meant for this' and recalls nights when he 'would get changed in the kitchen at the venues and walk through the crowd in his pyjamas.' He told a journalist it would save him time when he got home (150 miles away), then was overheard saying to the local lasses 'Ready for bed'?

Perhaps the final piece of the puzzle could now fall into place with a couple of high-profile shows, right in at the deep end where they knew they could prove themselves and their merit in the way they knew best. Supporting no-one and playing to an audience who could appreciate their achievements on their own merits, they headed for the Marquee in December 1982. This was no disappointment either as Nick Kemp of *Kerrang* was to find out. He reported 'Even my usually frequent sojourns to the bar were rendered impossible as my legs turned to jelly at the sheer excellence of this latest combo to hit these shores from the Emerald Isle.' This, he said, was down to a lethal combination of 'melody, sheer power, balls and instrumental finesse' which led him to conclude with some finality 'Mama's Boys will be one of the biggest things to hit the music business since the Stones and you can quote me on that.' Pippa Lang from *Metal Fury* also caught up with them at the Marquee gigs reporting that over 600 people had crammed in and that the venue had even had to turn people away. She invited her readers to ask the inevitable question 'Do you think perhaps they know this may be one of their last chances to see the boys in so small a place?' According to this critic, and a growing number of others, Mama's Boys had arrived.

What happened next, in Mike Mansfield's opinion, was the 'genius of Phil Lynott', hoisting them off a national stage and depositing them onto an international one. As a kid John had had the gatefold sleeve of Thin Lizzy's *Live and Dangerous* stuck to his bedroom wall -the last thing he would see before going to sleep at night and the first thing he would see in the morning. Pat had derived enormous inspiration from Brian Robertson's lead work in *Still in Love With You* from the same album which, to this day, he calls 'one of the finest solos I have ever heard.' Now, beyond even their own dreams, they were invited to open for Thin Lizzy on the *Thunder*

in ST. NINNIDH'S HALL
DERRYLIN
On SATURDAY, 16th APRIL

THIS IS THE VERY FIRST APPEARANCE OF THE BAND ON THEIR OWN HOME TERRITORY

Don't miss this chance to see the local lads who are on a brief stop-over of their tour with Thin Lizzy, which has been a phenomenal success for Mama's Boys. On numerous radio interviews, one with Alan Freeman on London Capital Radio, where he said not since the ZZ Pop did they meet with such versatility. The Press reviews have read:

"Make way for Mama's Boys" (Kerrang).
"Chockful of winners" (Noise).
"Teeming with fresh ideas" (Sounds).
"A notch above the rest" (Melody Maker).
And "The greatest things since the Rollings Stones" (Kerrang).

The renowned Marquee Club, where such names as the Beatles and Rolling Stones first made an impact, was a sell-out for Mama's Boys.

MAKE IT A SELL-OUT ON SATURDAY 16th IN DERRYLIN

These reports along with a major recording contract will take Mama's Boys to far off fields, so don't miss this chance to see them on the ground where they were born.

Admission £2.00 · Commencing 10 to 1.30
SUPPORT BAND "LIPSTICK"

Homecoming announcement: St. Ninnidh's Hall.

60

and Lightning Tour which was also to be the Irish legends' Farewell. As if passing the baton, Lynott chose to take Mama's Boys out on the road with him and, symbolically at least, in closing one career open another, just as Horslips had done. It was quite an endorsement and *Kerrang* was quick to pick up on the significance of it running a story called 'Boys From The Black Stuff. ' In this, the readership was informed with finality that the secret was now officially out: the band was a runaway success and this would be their breakthrough year.

Mama's Boys, who have just finished a highly successful tour with Thin Lizzy, are sure to be given a great welcome home when they play at St. Ninnidh's Hall, Derrylin, this Saturday, 16th April.

Homecoming picture: 'Mama's Boys will be one of the biggest things to hit the music business since the Stones, and you can quote me on that.'

When the McManus brothers actually met Phil Lynott properly in Scarborough, their idol turned out to be a fairly intimidating, and no-messing, kind of character, setting out his stall very clearly with a list of dos and don'ts. Pat remembers thinking that as long as they stuck to these guidelines everything would be fine, and so 'We were like "Yes, Mr Lynott, No, Mr Lynott". He was a superstar, and he was a gentle person, a lovely person with a heart of gold.' As the boys, all teetotal and anti-drugs, were unlikely to be causing much trouble, and as they worshipped the ground the lads from Lizzy walked on, Lynott needn't have bothered. Quite the contrary. Before long he realised that and, far from keeping them distant, used to hang around with them either offering advice to the up-and-comers or simply getting away from what he called the 'liggers' who were infesting his dressing room. As the Thin Lizzy band room was permanently full to the doors, and as the Mama's Boys one seemed to be equally impressively empty, he would seek refuge in there. John remembers Lynott would come in grumbling '"fuckin' people eating your food and nicking your clothes".' As the tour progressed they became friends to the point that Lynott could touch on a potentially raw nerve saying 'You need to take a bit of a look at how you dress on the stage. You can't be too different from the punter in the audience, but you need to have that little something so that the kid will look up and say "Ah fuck, I want that".' They remonstrated that while he could get all his clothes tailor-made for him they were still looking for bargains in Carnaby Street, but he wouldn't let it drop. Pushing on with 'these words of wisdom for about 20 minutes' he finally left to get ready for the show. Just before he went on, and within minutes of Mama's Boys getting back to their band room, he popped his head round the door and said 'John, can you give me the lend of your leg-warmers?'

With Joe Wynne however relations were not always so cordial as he was utterly determined to keep the brothers on their toes to maximise this touring experience. John remembers his shock one night just after they came off stage in Newcastle when

> He just grabbed me by the neck and put me up against the wall. He yelled 'If you ever fuckin' go out there and do another fuckin' show like that I'll kick your fuckin' arse!' It was quite a shock. I made bloody sure that every night I went on after that that I was paying attention to what I was doing.

Ironically John had noticed worrying inconsistencies not with his own band, but with his heroes. When Phil and his band were on form they

FRIDAY 26th AUGUST

the stranglers

MAN

STEEL PULSE

From Finland
HANOI ROCKS

PALLAS

SOLSTICE

PENDRAGON

AUTO DAFÉ

SPECIAL GUESTS
BIG COUNTRY

SATURDAY 27th AUGUST

BLACK SABBATH

MARILLION

SUZI QUATRO

MAGNUM

From Ireland
MAMA'S BOYS

HEAVY PETTIN'

LEE AARON

FORTUNE

CRAZY ANGEL

SPECIAL GUESTS from USA
STEVIE RAY VAUGHAN & DOUBLE TROUBLE

SPECIAL GUESTS **ANVIL** from Canada

SUNDAY 28th AUGUST

THIN LIZZY

SPECIAL GUESTS from USA
LITTLE STEVEN & THE DISCIPLES OF SOUL

STEVE HARLEY & COCKNEY REBEL

CLIMAX BLUES BAND

THE ENID

SAD CAFÉ

ONE THE JUGGLER

TWELFTH NIGHT

OPPOSITION

SPECIAL ATTRACTION
TEN YEARS AFTER

DJ's & Linkmen · Jerry Floyd · Mike Quinn & Martin Ball

Following Pettin' was no easy task but my first viewing of **Mamas Boys** *still* left a very pleasant dent in the mind. Three totally unassuming welcome variation on the HM theme with the best of 'em. Pat McManus' fiddle provided welcome variation on the HM theme and the band's songs are strong enough to ensure some kind of success. I'd say that some of their riffs sound a touch too familiar but experience will give 'em more of their own identity. The punters loved 'em and I for one wouldn't argue with that!

or through usual local coach companies.

£5.95

NB: OUR CAMPSITE IS RESERVED FOR WEEKEND TICKET HOLDERS ONLY.

The Reading Festival: 'A three-day binge of booze, mud and decibels.'

63

were unbeatable, but sometimes a more sinister and destructive side could emerge that did the music, and the musicians, no good at all. Talking of these swings he remembers

> There were nights where he wasn't in the greatest of moods as he was doing all sorts of stuff on that tour and a lot of the lads in Lizzy were also. But on the nights when he was in good form he was just a great, great friend, gave us a lot of guidance, and was very kind to us.

John Sykes, fresh in from the Tygers of Pan Tang, remembers the brothers being innocent and awestruck, 'young and happy to be there, as was I.' John McManus, in return, remembers Sykes with enormous admiration, but with a caveat too, saying he was 'a great little guitarist' who 'unfortunately was on an awful, ridiculous' road to self destruction. And although Scott Gorham was a 'lovely, really lovely' guy, he had the same problems. John reflects 'When they were clean you just couldn't compete,' but when they were not, like in Leeds in front of 15,000 punters, 'they were shit.' Thin Lizzy, their all-time musical heroes, were jeopardizing so much talent at the hands of a rampant, seemingly uncontrollable, drug use. In Scandinavia (with Abba watching from the side-stage) things went from bad to worse. Terrible rows began as Phil yelled at John Sykes to stop while there was still time, knowing in all probability that he had ruined his own life with the same reckless behaviour. John remembers that this side of the rock world in which they now found themselves had no appeal for them whatsoever, in fact it disgusted them: 'You see it and you don't go "That looks nice". It didn't look nice. It looked seedy and horrible.' As for himself 'I never felt the need to look for anything else as I was getting everything I wanted out of the music and being in a band.' Anyway, nobody had ever said that Lynott and his band were perfect role models and the fact remained they were idolised for their music.

On the entire tour the three brothers only missed seeing Lizzy from the side of the stage at one show in Oxford when they were called off to do an interview. John laughs about it now saying they were so star-struck they didn't even miss the opening moments when the house lights went down and the atmosphere became electric in anticipation of the arrival of Lizzy. This was what rock n' roll was, not all that other stuff. When the tour made its way into Belfast and Dublin Mama's Boys were well into their stride. Far from intimidated, during a wind-swept BBC interview outside the Kings Hall, Tommy wouldn't stop acting the lig, leaving Pat to try and hold it together and to speak sensibly on behalf of the band. With

Pat live at Reading (published in Kerrang*): 'It felt as though we had at last been accepted by the people who matter the most.'*

Pat with the Reading crowd: 'Next round! Can you stick the bottles?'

Finalé at Reading: 'The punters loved 'em and I for one wouldn't argue with that!'

The brothers backstage at Reading: 'These guys are going places and for once in rock's erratic life, here's a band that deserves every ounce of the acclaim they're about to receive.'

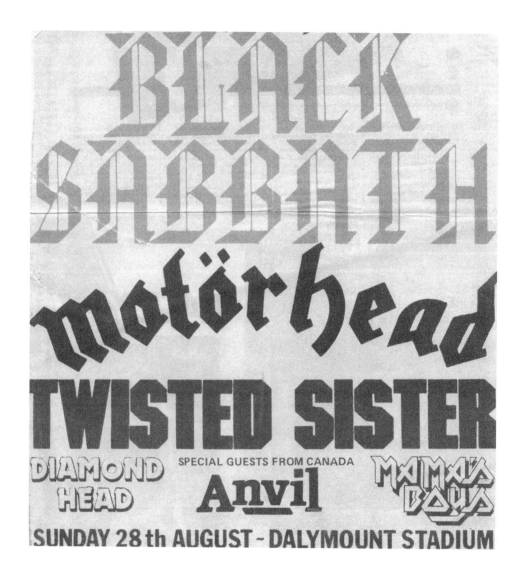

Dalymount Festival: 'They stole the show [and] made Motörhead and Black Sabbath look like the ageing old hippies they really are'

grim determination, and a stifled smile, he reported honestly 'It is just up to us to get out there and prove ourselves, which we've done. We've had a tremendous reaction to the whole tour.' Big John and Valerie were invited too. After the Horslips racket in Belturbet this was their first big rock concert and a chance to see what all the hard work by their boys had been for. Valerie remembers seeing them up there in front of a packed stadium, with the crowd singing along to every note they played, and concludes 'We were so proud. It was just magical. I'll remember it until the day I die.'

Not sufficiently star-struck yet they also took time out from the Lizzy trek to go home to Fermanagh, not for a well earned rest, but to play a small concrete hall with a corrugated iron roof in Derrylin for the locals. Advertised as a 'homecoming' in the county press there was a widespread realisation that this really was the very, very last chance to see the boys in such a place. And so in a church hall, with the amateur dramatics stage set still in place behind them, the punters present knew that this final glimpse was priceless. John concludes with a backward glance 'Before going on tour with Lizzy we thought we knew it all, but really we knew nothing. It was an honour to play with them and an incredible experience.' By the time the Lizzy tour wound up 'We had gone from being an unknown band to being able to sell out three nights in a row at the Marquee in London. That was the difference it made. We have Lizzy to thank for that.' There would be no more church halls from here on in.

At around this time a story broke in the press that Pat had been offered Bernie Marsden's place in Whitesnake. Pat remembers how this came about

> I think we had been looking to do a tour with Whitesnake but they wanted to hear the album first. So Coverdale listened to the album then got the office to contact me with the message that they didn't think anyone was playing guitar like that anymore.

David Coverdale now sought to extricate the talented guitarist from the three-piece, as Dio had done with Vivian Campbell from Sweet Savage. Far from euphoric and packing his case to board the first plane to stardom, Pat dismissed the whole offer as 'a nice compliment' then reiterated clearly 'but I wouldn't have left.' In *Sounds* he was quizzed further about it and admitted that while it was 'a great compliment to my playing. I would never leave the boys for £1 million. They're my brothers.' If anyone had needed reminding of the unpretentious nature of the band, of the sincere desire to create only good music, and of their absolute belief in their ability to succeed together,

Pat with Dee Snider (Twisted Sister) in Dublin: 'A bit frightening at first, but a nicer bunch of guys you could never meet.'

John and Tommy backstage at Dalymount: 'Clearly the days when Thin Lizzy could lay claim to being the unchallenged kings of Irish hard rock are not numbered, they are over.'

here it was in spades. Whitesnake would have to do without Pat McManus and so turned to Mel Galley. Pat winds the story up saying 'Years later Tommy met him [David Coverdale] in the Whisky [a-go-go in LA], and Coverdale remembered it well and said "Your brother is the only person who ever, ever, ever turned down the gig". '

The next triumph for Joe Wynne was getting the unsigned Mama's Boys onto the bill for the last ever Reading Rock Festival at the Thameside Arena site. Described in the advertisement as a 'three-day binge of booze, mud and decibels' this had always been a Mecca for hard rock music and a venue that any band without a record deal was very unlikely to get a shot at. Now Mama's Boys were on the bill on the same day as Black Sabbath, Marillion, Magnum and Suzi Quatro. The previous day Hanoi Rocks and The Stranglers had been there, and interestingly enough, so had Steel Pulse (who had instigated their name change several years back). The following day the festival would be brought to a triumphant finalé by Thin Lizzy. Anticipating the event and how the McManus brothers would take the opportunity to get their message across to 30,000 music lovers, one Irish journalist warned 'Mama's Boys' performance at Reading could provide a fierce battle for their rivals. After being bottled up in the studio for three months, the cork should blow with a bang. '

Flying in from Ireland a little late, they arrived at the site just in time to see Anvil being bottled off the stage amidst a storm of cat calls and abuse. The Canadians had managed, with their spandex, bondage gear and attitude, to wind the crowd up a treat and so when Lips (singer and guitarist) walked past John to leave the stage he said 'Man, we have to change our name to 'cANned-VILle. ' Heavy Pettin' were next and went down a bit better but nevertheless Pat told a journalist 'It was terrifying before we went on because there was a guy cleaning all the cans from the stage. It was a case of "Next round! Can *you* stick the bottles?"' Then, just as they went on to play the most important set of their lives, John remembers a lull in the battle 'They never threw anything at us. I was amazed. ' With the fragile truce in place the band could focus on getting the job done right, which, quite frankly was no problem at all. Pat looks back on it now and says that once the riot had died down his only nerves emanated from much closer to home

I was more worried about what the lads would say, or the dirty look, or the kick in the ass from John. It never entered my head to be nervous, other than thinking I better do this right or Tommy will get stuck into me after the gig, or John would give out stink 'What the fuck was all that about?' That's what I was worried about.

He needn't have worried though as their unpretentious personas and well polished tunes (including an extended barn dance fiddle solo at the end of *Demon*) won the crowd over convincingly. A *Kerrang* reporter observed 'The punters loved 'em and I for one wouldn't argue with that!' Another noted that they had given 'a stunning performance that brought the first deserved encore of the weekend.' Derek Oliver went further and said they were the highlight of the entire weekend and that the combination of 'power-packed boogie, blitzing axe attack and memorable songs' combined with 'traditional-tongue-in-cheek Irish blarney in their lyrics' had lead quite simply to a quality performance from a class act. The review continued to gush 'Pat "The Professor" is shaping up to be a another master axeman much in the Angus Young style of crank it up and blow yer face out overkill', then finished with 'These guys are going places and for once in rock's erratic life, here's a band that deserves every ounce of the acclaim they're about to receive.' Tommy Vance played their entire set on the Friday Rock Show and added his name to the ever-growing list of believers, while *Melody Maker* marked 'their arrival as a major force, eclipsing virtually every other set of the weekend.' With time to think over their achievement and the importance of that one performance, Pat reflects

> Reading was great and the audience was so good to us. It was honestly one of the most emotional gigs we've played as the crowd was going nuts during the whole set. It felt as though we had at last been accepted by the people who matter the most.

To this day John says he will never forget the sight or sound of 30,000 people singing 'Straight forward, no looking back' -something which was 'just phenomenal.'

The roller coaster ride didn't stop there either and the very next day Mama's Boys opened the Dalymount Festival in Ireland in front of 6,000 people where, according to Cathal Dervan, 'they stole the show [and] made Motörhead and Black Sabbath look like the ageing old hippies they really are.' He went on to observe that 'with their loyal horde of Irish followers treating every song as if it were their national anthem' Mama's Boys could not lose. The OTT performances of Twisted Sister ('all the finesse of a J. C. B. demolishing a Morris Minor') combined with the sheer musical class of Mama's Boys, left very little room for anyone else. Who could not resist the foul mouthed, over made up, arrogant showmanship of Dee Snider, teamed up with the musical brilliance (shrouded in humility) of

Mama's Boys? Snider himself was blown away and got his photograph taken with Pat for *Kerrang* in, of all places, the Lord Mayor of Dublin's office. Pat recalls that the two of them had been selected to represent the festival and so went dutifully saying 'You can imagine what that looked like.' That said, Pat knew right away that behind all the make up and the extreme language 'He was a business man Dee, he knew what he was doing. He was a very clever guy.' John remembers that Twisted Sister in general 'were a bit frightening at first, but a nicer bunch of guys you could never meet.' Next up Mama's Boys were booked in for the *Enfer* sponsored Sunshine Festival in Mulhouse, France on September 11, with Diamond Head, Blue Oyster Cult and the now familiar stable mates Black Sabbath, Twister Sister and Anvil but, ironically enough, the Sunshine Festival got rained off.

And yet for all of these large shows and for all the heady company they were now keeping, Mama's Boys also kept plodding away in places like the Russell Hotel in Navan, not only to keep local support stirred up but also to get themselves into tip-top shape for their first headlining tour of the UK promoting the new LP *Turn it up*. Pat reiterated, 'Ireland is still where the beans are' but observed a kind of laid back attitude in its audiences that worked on the principle that 'I'll see them next time round.' Now with major success virtually assured, and a possible imminent relocation to America, how many more 'next times' could there be? Journalist Cathal Dervan agreed saying 'Whether Ireland stands up and pays attention to this band before it is too late and they're gone is another story. Life begins at the top.'

But this twilight zone existence was in a kind of no-mans-land, somewhere between the Hammersmith Odeon and the rural halls in the west of Ireland. One night there would be the music critics gathered to make or break this new band, and the next it would be a bewildered handful of locals who didn't know the first thing about rock music, and almost certainly didn't like it either. The gulf was noticeable from 30,000 cheering punters at Reading to a few dozen geriatrics out for a 'dance' a couple of nights later; from the rock stars with Lizzy and Twisted Sister, to 'the band' at the ballroom being asked to play Big Tom. Years later Pat still laughs at the recollection of stubbornly taking this hard rock music to the rural parts of Ireland where

> they really didn't understand. 90% of them would go because there was a gig on, and they'd go to meet their future wives. I remember them trying to waltz or quickstep to *Gentlemen Rogues* one night and the sweat was blinding them.

Despite his protests that *In the Heat of the Night* and *Crazy Daisy's* were not 'straight-forward down-the-line bash-a-boogie' and were in fact quite danceable, few agreed. That didn't stop them trying though and Pat could see from the stage the farmers 'swingin' away and yer man out shaking his stuff. ' So while the critics marvelled at the sophistication of the 'ethnic heavy metal boogie attack', the people at the dance halls would have seen this as a foreign language and a very loud incomprehensible one at that. At other times the band itself ended up providing the laughs especially when on one occasion the road crew felt that the stage was a bit small compared to the giant ones they were rapidly becoming accustomed to. Accordingly they shoved the large flight cases all along the front of the stage and put the monitors on them to give an extra few feet. The cases were, of course, on wheels and so when Pat leapt forward onto one of the monitors to strike a dramatic pose in anticipation of an impending solo, it rolled off into the audience with him on board. The crowd parted like the Red Sea and Pat sailed on towards the back of the hall equally red faced.

Regarding what to release confidence was also building in the Mama's Boys camp to the point that they could even consider overruling the decisions of executives at RTE and other broadcasting groups. With a strongly implied, and almost painfully naïve, 'Up yours!' they handed the radio companies a copy of *Loose Living*, a taster for the new album, which predictably enough then didn't get played. With that came the sobering reality that without radio play a band, any band, was 'stone dead. 'With one eye on the commercial market and the other on musical integrity, therefore, they realised they couldn't say 'up yours' to too many more people.

Phil Lynott and the boys from Thin Lizzy kept in touch with the McManus brothers after The Farewell Tour. On one occasion when Lizzy were at Polydor studios mixing *Live / Life* they made a promise to call in at the Marquee to see Mama's Boys on one of their three sold out shows. Though they had not dared to expect it the brothers had nevertheless hoped for the Lizzy lads to keep their promise and 'were absolutely gutted' when, as the night wore on, nobody showed up. John picks up the story 'A week afterwards we were in Nottingham and during the sound check in walked Phil, John Sykes and Mark Stanway. I nearly cacked myself. I couldn't believe it. Fuckin' Lynott walking up towards me!' Phil explained to him 'We felt bad about not being able to get to the Marquee so we just though fuck it, y'know, we'll come up to Nottingham, tonight. ' John remembers being blown away by the fact that they would go to such an effort to make amends calling it a 'Lovely thing to do, they didn't have

The boys promoting new sponsors, Lee: 'A new era in Irish rock music was born.'

Publicity photos for Turn it up: 'I am now going to get well loaded, stick my head in between the speakers and become the rock and roll hero I'd almost forgotten about.'

Advertising the Turn it up *tour: 'Mama's Boys are very good now and can only become awesomely good.'*

to do it. ' And so at the tail end of an already exhausting one day festival at the Sherwood Rooms which had seen Witchfynde, Hell and Shy Wolf go through their paces, an Irish jam began in front of a crowd that simply could not get enough. Dave Dickson felt differently and told the readers of *Kerrang* that the jam of *A Day in the Life of a Blues Singer, Cold Sweat* and *Baby Drives Me Crazy*, did Mama's Boys no good at all: 'A get-together it was not – a *coup* it most certainly was. ' He finished up by making certain candid suggestions amongst which was the fact that Pat needed to ditch the Jimmy Page histrionics on the guitar and realise that 'They are not yet in a position to be able to cope with this kind of competition … basically they allowed themselves to be walked over!' Sean Naylor from *Hot Press* shared none of this pessimism and concluded impressively 'Clearly the days when Thin Lizzy could lay claim to being the unchallenged kings of Irish hard rock are not numbered, they are over. '

Kerrang announce the arrival of *Mama's Boys.*

Runaway Dreams live in Omagh: 'Live you can't argue with us. When we go on stage we give every ounce of energy that we can possibly pull out of the bag.'

Horsing around in America: 'Ah well you see we were being taught by the elder statesmen on how to behave'.

Michael Deeney and Damian McCollum in America: 'They could have been successful all over the world, not just in America. They could have sold out Wembley.'

Chapter 3: Mama's Boys Come of Age

As all the early indicators had suggested, the new album, *Turn it up*, hit the spot. Barry Devlin was at the helm again with Philip Begley, Jim Lockhart and Don Baker there to make sure the finished product captured the increasingly identifiable Mama's Boys 'sound. 'With the luxury of three weeks in the studio this time, as opposed to rushing through the whole process with one eye on the clock and the other on the cheque book, Pat remembers thinking 'We have at last been treated like a real band. ' The cover of the LP exuded a confidence, or at least a direction, that had not been there before either, even if John remembers 'We were worried what our mum and dad were going to think. 'The semi-topless 'rock chick', complete with white leather mini-skirt, bullet belt and Bono shades, was certainly more eye catching than the blank white sleeve of the *Official Bootleg* or the Iron Maiden style writing on a black background of *Plug it in*. Opening out the inside sleeve of the LP it became apparent that the lyrics had got a lot more risqué too, talking as they did about dens of ill repute, rogues on the prowl, and loose living. Pat bashfully recalls this with an element of discomfort

> The lyrical content was really always a problem to me because I wasn't that way inclined at all. You can have a vivid imagination, but mine was in the music. I could write riffs until the cows come home, then think, the dreaded lyrics now.

In accompanying promotional photos the boys were also clearly plugging their new sponsors, Lee. This seemingly random deal had been struck when Peter Kerr, hitching a lift to the Kings Hall, had been picked up by George Graham, an executive from the denim company. On the way there Kerr had convinced Graham to come to the show during which the latter had become an instant convert and struck a sponsorship deal on the spot. That was the way business was done in those days. Soon there was talk that a major Japanese motorbike company might become sponsors too, and so the new tour posters featured the lads with some brand new machines which, in reality, were way out of their price league. On a personal and deeply poignant note, the brothers dedicated the album to their sister Valerie who would have reveled so much in this success.

And the music? That was the real triumph. In an article called 'Boys Will Be Boys' Derek Oliver noted that Mama's Boys were getting ever nearer to knowing exactly what they wanted from their tunes and that Barry Devlin and Philip Begley were masters in assisting them to do so. The energy and originality of *Plug it in* was undoubtedly still there but now harnessed to an emerging range and sophistication which was, in turn, providing the 'quantum leap' needed to propel them to 'astonishing maturity.' Neil Jeffries noted how diversity reined supreme, from the bluesy harmonica on the ZZ Top inspired *Lonely Soul*, through the commercial potential of the semi-ballad *Too Little of You to Love*, to the trade mark fiddle on *Freedom Fighters*. In the latter Pat seemed to amalgamate the musically complex structure of *Runaway Dreams* with the lyrical philosophy of *Belfast City Blues* to create perhaps the high point of the album. Or perhaps it was the unfettered axe work in *Gentlemen Rogues* that led Jay Williams to conclude his review saying that 'Pat is, at the moment, a better guitarist than Michael Schenker', on a par with Eddie Van Halen, and neck-in-neck with fellow countryman Vivian Campbell. Another observer noted with pleasure that Pat was more interested 'in harmonics than histrionics', and so had created 'lavishly embellished, well structured, lead solos. ' Sean Naylor claimed that *Crazy Daisy's House of Dreams* contained 'the riff of '83', (another critic had called it 'a riff chunkier and meatier than a can of Pedigree Chum') then signed off with the advice 'Turn it up! Full Blast. ' *Turn it up* had its critics too, notably back in Dublin where *Hot Press* said of one of their singles 'Throw it into the bin with the rest of the Gary Moore rubbish. ' Pat took 'lying in the bin next to Gary Moore' as a compliment but still wondered why Irish journalists knocked local bands instead of supporting them. Elsewhere another reviewer of the new single *Too Little of You to Love* conceded 'Now these boys certainly brought a smile of enjoyment to my face at Reading this year, but I'm afraid this record was wiped it clean off.' Closer to home Cathal Dervan wasn't having any of that and concluded definitively that these songs 'are to be written into the history of Irish rock as classics of their kind. '

If the album reviews had been excellent then the reports of its performance live were exemplary. A warm up show at the claustrophobic Baggott Inn in Dublin left one critic saying that he had 'the feeling I was witnessing a phenomenon. I thoroughly advise you to partake of the experience. ' Champing at the bit to get on the road and capitalize on the momentum they had built up with Thin Lizzy, a sixteen date UK tour to promote *Turn it up* was soon under way. Perhaps on paper the timing might not have seemed so great with Dio, Y&T, Ozzy and Michael Schenker all out on the circuit at that time too, but it seemed to make very little difference as the halls were full every night. After playing support to long-time hero Johnny Winter at the Hammersmith Odeon, Mama's Boys took off on their own causing the audience, in tandem with the potential of the band itself, to go 'completely berserk.' Pat agreed that things had certainly changed since that initial frosty reception on the Hawkwind Tour, yet reiterated his ethos of playing for the love of it, saying 'We'll put the same effort into playing even if we're the only people in the place. I can't stand all this seriousness, it spoils the atmosphere.' He went on 'Live you can't argue with us. When we go on stage we give every ounce of energy that we can possibly pull out of the bag.' Another thing singling the McManus brothers out from many of their peers was their sense of altruism to other musicians, journalists and fans, and this caused Pippa Lang to write 'Thank God – no hot aired balloon heads here', just a few nice guys who were dreaming of getting to Japan 'to try their luck out there.' Other reports also cherished the fact that they had kept their feet firmly on the ground with no 'daddy cool' antics, and noted that they had even retained their strong Fermanagh accents. Jay Williams wrote a *Sounds* article called 'Your Mama Wouldn't Like It! From Shamrock to Wham Rock, the Story of Ireland's Mama's Boys', in which he asked rhetorically 'But what is this? A real guitar hero who smiles?' Despite Dante Bonutto's recollection that the early 1980s was the time when 'rock was at its most excessive, outrageous, decadent, stupid, all the great things, the iconic things, about rock', Pat remembers that far from throwing televisions from bedroom windows 'We were the only band that ever tidied a hotel before we left. We left the room prim and proper.' The hotel managers would see them off with 'You're the best band we've had in here. Jesus, you've even made the beds.' (One year later a photograph was taken of a wrecked room in America on the Ratt and Twisted Sister Tour of 1984 to which Pat bashfully pleads no contest, offering in his defense only 'Ah well you see we were being taught by the elder statesmen on how to behave.') It was not an inconsequential fact that the McManus boys made friends and won respect wherever they went. The music may well have been blistering rock n' roll played at break neck speed, but it was written and performed by talented and genuine lads from Fermanagh, not the arrogant and abusive misfits more normally associated with the genre. One critic concluded 'From a hesitant, over-cautious little ensemble, the McManus brothers have thrown restraint to the wind and matured into a proverbial ball of fire.' Brian Harrigan agreed and signed off his review acknowledging that the trip had only just begun and that 'Mama's Boys are very good now and can only become awesomely good.'

Though it was the last thing on their minds at the time, there would soon have to be some serious talk of a record deal. As *Turn it up* (like the two albums before it) had been self financed, as the unsigned band had taken the stage at Lisdoonvarna, Reading and Dalymount to great acclaim, and as they had also escorted Thin Lizzy around northern Europe on such a prestigious tour, it was surely time for some major label support. John shrugs 'We didn't pursue a record deal at all, just the assistance of distributors, until late in 1983 when record companies started coming to see us. ' The boys had always been happy to generate an income through intensive touring and selling records and T-shirts at gigs. Now, however, realizing that the next step might very well hoist them onto a world stage, they faced up to the unsavory fact that they had to think a little less about music and a little more about the pragmatics of the music industry. To do this they sought additional managerial help from ex-Horslips and Murray Head manager Michael Deeney. Barry Devlin had already forced him to go to Ireland to see the boys in action with the result that 'what I saw in some pub blew me away. ' He remembers the band was 'Blues based hard rock music, in the line of Rory Gallagher and Thin Lizzy,' while Pat was 'an exceptional guitarist and a very special talent. ' Managerially, Michael was not being asked to take over completely from Joe Wynne, but to work beside him to land an international record deal for which he would get a percentage. Michael remembers 'At that point in my career I had quite a few contacts which gets you past the first hurdle of the record company actually listening to the band. 'These contacts were all over the world and could definitely lead to decent exposure, especially in America. Michael also worried that Joe had taken the band down a very 'heavy metal' road in marketing which he felt to be 'all wrong. ' Simultaneously, the brothers themselves were beginning to get the nagging suspicion that the higher they went the further Joe was getting out of his depth. Bartering and scrapping around Ireland and the UK, John remembers 'He was great', but now as the band was becoming fully international and the type of people associated with it changed from dance hall owners to corporate types in suits 'he was canceling out all of it out by upsetting a lot of really important people. ' But that is not a fair reflection of their career together to that point and so John hurriedly emphasizes that 'Everything Joe did from the very beginning right up the very end he did 100% -there's no two ways about that. '

The promised record deal was not long in coming. Far from the glittering offices of central London and the corporate world of contracts and lawyers, the deal was clinched following a few pots of tea and a plate of sandwiches in Derrylin. Mama's Boys were signed to the fledgling Jive (who would later sign Britney Spears) on the promise that the legendary Mutt Lange (of

Pat and Chris Tsangerides (CT) recording Mama's Boys.

Live after the release of Mama's Boys: *'In the UK it is all the long hair, the leather jacket with the arse of the trousers all ripped ... metal fans.'*

AC/DC and Def Leppard fame) would produce their next record. For this reason alone they turned down Geffen, who already had Mötley Crüe and would soon sign Guns n' Roses. The executives liked the idea that Mama's Boys was not a 'manufactured band' but had grown organically from sheer talent and hard work, and now only needed a bit of support. Perhaps with a tweak or two here and there, and with some heightened publicity, there would soon be an international rock band on the road as opposed to a local heavy metal one. To this day Michael Deeney still shares Jive's original enthusiasm when he reiterates 'They could have been successful all over the world, not just in America. They could have sold out Wembley.'

If 1983 had finished on a high note, then 1984 started with promise in equal measure as Mama's Boys hit the road with the Scorpions. Riding high on the success of *Blackout* and now promoting the new opus *Love at First Sting*, the Scorpions had scheduled an extensive trip through the UK and France. Mama's Boys were invited to join them and so released the single *Midnight Promises* and *Lonely Soul* to coincide with the outing. Though the McManus boys didn't glean too much musically from a nightly study of their mentors, they realized that they certainly had a lot to learn from them about the music business and the sheer professionalism required to stay popular, productive and profitable. John remembers that they were so methodical and would have a precisely allocated time for a picture shoot, then the discipline of having only one drink back at the hotel before bed. Additionally, they owned their own buses, lighting companies and everything else that would have cost them money on the road had they been renting. Even in their performances John remembers 'You never saw the Scorpions play a bad show.' Not even in England where the venues were too small to house their full stage and equipment requirements. In terms of publicity, the tour certainly did Mama's Boys no harm at all and if anything the Scorpions soon came to the bitter / sweet realization that they really had a 'live' opening act. Jay Williams, reviewing the Hammersmith gig, even suggested that Mama's Boys had come out on top. In France too the competition was obvious for all to see, especially at the Palais Omnisports de Bercy in Paris, where 17,000 frantic punters kept calling Mama's Boys back for encores and in their ensuing enthusiasm caused extensive damage to the brand new venue. The reception was unheard of for a support band and so one French journalist who witnessed the event earmarked the 29th of February 1984 as a historic day, not only because Mama's Boys were the first band ever to play in the fabulous arena, but because they had given the Scorpions such a run for their money. Perhaps coincidentally when the main act took to the stage singer Klaus Meine developed health problems a mere fifteen minutes into the set and collapsed, fuelling rumors that they had not cared for the competition. John dismisses any such conspiracy theories and concludes honestly 'The Scorpions never had anything to worry about from us.' On the contrary, and to give them their due, the Scorpions happily extended an invitation to the brothers to keep going with them all the way across the arenas of the USA when Europe was finished. Knowing that sold-out stadiums and festivals awaited, that the Scorpions were at the top of their game, and that MTV was already pushing them as hard as they could, John recalls 'it was a tough one to turn down.' In the eyes of the record company however it would have been jumping the gun as Mama's Boys didn't yet have any marketable recordings or videos to help break them in when they got there. Touring the USA was not going to be cheap and so would need meticulous planning to ensure that the assault would succeed on the first attempt. The executives at Jive therefore suggested that the boys get into the studio, get a solid LP recorded (and very possibly a hit single), and leave the USA until there was something tangible to market. There would be plenty more opportunities to tour in the future.

With the ink scarcely dry on the contract therefore the label booked them in for some serious recording time with legend Chris Tsangarides (of Thin Lizzy, Iron Maiden, Judas Priest and Y&T fame) at London's Battery Studios. Tsangerides himself, fully aware of the potential he was working with, demonstrated his complete commitment to the project by going across to Fermanagh and basing himself at The Shed in Derrylin while rehearsals were underway. Taking notes, throwing in some keyboard ideas, and planning out how best to approach the recording of this band, he was soon bowled over by the lads with whom he instantly developed a 'very good working relationship.' Pat, he felt, was 'a really great musician, John was the image and 'the shape thrower' but not an egoist, and Tommy had such vibrancy for life.' He also understood very clearly that for all they were each admirable in their own way, together they exuded a strength and coherence that only telepathy shared by three siblings could bring about.

The finished LP, simply called *Mama's Boys*, was packaged with the prevailing trends of America in mind and was intended as a 'catch up' for those potential fans who had not as yet had a chance to hear the best bits of the first three records. Tsangarides remembered that 'we had upped the ante' but in doing so had had to strip the work of its original atmosphere in order to remarket it. Also, into the mix was thrown a strategically chosen new single in the form of Slade classic *Mama We're All Crazee Now*. This,

'Boy Wonders': 'The whole hair brigade was pure theatre, we were in show business, it was entertainment. We thought of ourselves as artists, we never thought that we had to be entertainers as well.'

it was certain, would be lapped up by the American market and give the all-important breakthrough if the re-vamped *Needle in the Groove* didn't. Michael Deeney still believes that *Needle in the Groove* should have done the trick and remains bewildered why it did not. Perhaps it arrived too early in their career when nobody was really paying attention, meaning that every subsequent reincarnation was simply a rehash of a perfectly good original. To have an imminently catchy and toe tapping backup then did make complete sense.

John remembers that it was Clive Calder's (the owner of Jive Records) idea to record *Mama We're All Crazee Now*. Tsangerides agreed, giving his full support and appreciating that strategically it was precisely what was required of a band at that stage in its career. His memory of it is simple: 'It was the 1980s, that's what you needed to do.' Even though it was not the sort of song, or even the sort of band, that Mama's Boys would normally have been into, when Calder would put his head round the door at the studio and ask 'Did you manage to take a look at the Slade track?' John remembers 'We felt bad that we hadn't even listened to.' Pat also recounts how casually they approached the potentially vital project.

> Chris Tsangirides said 'Okay let's hear the version of *Mama We're All Crazee Now*' to which I replied 'I don't even know the song.' He said 'You're kidding. That is what this whole vision is hanging on.' I said 'Well what key is it in? Is this okay'? And John said 'Aye that'll do the best' and we tore into it. And that was about as much respect as we had for that song. Get it out of the way.

Next Tsangerides and John (nicknaming themselves The Shapettes) got to work creating the catchy stadium vocals by re-recording themselves 'about a million times from different positions in the studio' to create 'a stomp along chorus' which America would surely love. When it was done it sounded great -not much like the Mama's Boys the purists had grown up on -but great nonetheless. It also brought into focus a wider debate that would play itself out fully over the coming years. How do you differentiate good management and marketing decisions from being pulled and pushed in directions that nobody had never previously thought of going? A cynic might well ask whether or not it was really necessary to try and break the band on a cover version of an old song with a gimmicky connection in the title, as opposed to promoting their own highly original material which had taken them this far. In retrospect Pat knows that 'they should have let us develop as we were developing ... but that wasn't the case, they were looking

The Marquee: 'Mama we're all stone deaf now.'

Mama's Boys with Noddy Holder (Slade) who 'couldn't get onto the stage.'

for instant returns. ' John shares the skepticism about recording covers and even re-recording previously released numbers like *Needle in the Groove* and *Straight Forward.*

> This is where you start to feel uncomfortable about having a record deal. You completely lose control. The last thing you want to do is go in and re-record something you have already done. For me there were real danger signs flashing for our career. The record company still seemed to be depending on this one song we had written way back at the beginning of our career.

The LP sleeve too was, in the boys opinion, unsatisfactory and yet they felt powerless to do anything much about it. Pat remembers

> You take whatever they give you and you go with it. You can throw a tantrum and a fit but in their eyes you are being awkward. That was the last thing we wanted. We couldn't afford to do that. We were afraid to go in and say we don't like this.

Naïve of the industry, and grateful for the interest that was being shown in them, the brothers went along with just about everything that was sent their way.

When the pre-release tape was sent to reviewers and critics none of these tensions, frustrations or uncertainties was evident at all. Instead the music did the talking, boasting diversity, originality and sheer professionalism. The bluesy *Lonely Soul* had been totally made over and now benefited from backup vocals from the girl band Rock Goddess, an additional harmonica solo, and a guitar solo from Pat which came perilously close to *Fool For Your Stockings* by ZZ Top. There was also a welcomed showcase for Pat in the form of an instrumental called *The Professor* which left no-one in any doubt at all about the range and talent of this guitarist. Jay Williams happily gave the LP five stars and wound up saying 'Having appreciated it on aesthetic criteria, I am now going to get well loaded, stick my head in between the speakers and become the rock and roll hero I'd almost forgotten about. ' One dissenting voice came from Dave Sinclair who felt the whole LP to be a bit of a yawn for everyone who already knew the band and who didn't really want to see any high-tech tampering with the original songs. He did allow however that for the rest of the world to catch / wake up there could be a brief pause in the march to stardom. Thousands of miles away in America, Ozzy Osbourne's guitarist Jake E. Lee had taken to the album enthusiastically too and was playing it on the tour bus every night, catching the attention of keyboardist Don Airey. A decade later Airey would tour as the keyboardist in Mama's Boys.

Live, and now equipped with company funded state-of-the-art gear, a new backdrop with moving eyes, lasers, dry ice machines, a new lighting rig and an ever-growing crew to make all of this possible, Mama's Boys were definitely getting the label support they had always deserved. Tommy had a gigantic Ludwig drum kit and Pat and John were armed with complimentary Washburn guitars and a new backline. They also had had a bit of a make-over themselves with the old Lee T-shirts being binned in favor of waistcoats, leather pants and even new haircuts. First it was off to France for a headlining tour to satisfy their rapidly growing fan base there and to prove the critics right who had projected 'Mama's Boys Deviendront Grands.'

At the airport: 'Mama's Boys Deviendront Grands'.

Sprite **PRESENTS**

QUBE
MTV WELCOME!

A Heavy Metal Massacre!

RATT

RATT
TWISTED SISTER

Live In Concert

With Special Guest **MAMA'S BOYS**

TWISTED SISTER

Tickets on sale JUNE 30

Monday
July 30•7:30 PM
The Coliseum

The first American Tour with Ratt and Twisted Sister: 'You know this time last year we were playing gigs in Navan and Drogheda.'

Pat and John with Stephen Pearcey (Ratt): 'It was a mutual admiration. We got on really well with Ratt.'

93

Journalist Bruno Khaled was mesmerized by what he witnessed and spoke for thousands when he wrote of the dichotomy that was their fighting spirit and humble nature; the inherent beauty and implicit violence in both their music and their home nation; and the generosity and ferocity running simultaneously through the story of the Irish band. France took to Mama's Boys and in return the band played in almost as many remote corners of that country as ever they had done in Ireland. Then it was back to Ireland itself to hammer out a few dates with Samson who were eclipsed entirely by 'the rise and rise of the McManus brothers' in the 'white heat' of 'interstellar overdrive.' Mark Prendergast was one of many commentators who knew that America was now waiting, that Japan could not be far behind and then, without a doubt 'world domination' would follow. The journalists and critics lined up to heap their positive reviews and predictions on the band and so, after a show at the Saint Frances Xavier Hall in Dublin, one reported with finality 'a new era in Irish rock music was born.' Sean Naylor from *Hot Press* told his readers that if they did not know that Mama's Boys were the next big thing then they must have been 'working with Riley in Saudi Arabia.' *Sounds'* readers had voted them in at number 5 on the Best New Act category for 1983 and *Kerrang* readers now hoisted them to number 4 in the same category in 1984. Even the typically begrudging Irish music press rallied round the local-boys-turned-good and got to work sensationalizing their story with rumors of a 'seven figure record deal' which they had just landed. The newspapers blared 'Boys Strike Gold', quoting an immediate £30,000 for a new video, £130,000 which they had been paid up front for two records in one year with the possibility of an extension, taking the worldwide value of the band to approximately £1million. Perhaps, even with a hint of pride, they informed the readers that this was 'one of the largest contracts given to rock acts in the last six years.' There was no doubt about it -overnight the McManus brothers had been placed on a roller coaster of a career that involved huge sums of money, lawyers, contracts, jargon and all of it was making Pat, for one, very uneasy.

> That's when it became slightly scary as well. I used to just sit there and observe these businessmen talking, all round a table, the head of this and the head of that. There was a whole new pressure. They were all getting a wage out of it. It all started to get too much. And a lot of it fell on my shoulders because I was the oldest and possibly because I was writing as well. The fun was starting to disappear out of it.

Something else was causing concern too. For all the hype, publicity and new-found fame, very little money was filtering down as far as the brothers.

It seemed that for all they were getting massive logistical support and selling out halls every night, they were still fundamentally broke. The Ford Transit, loaded up with eight people (more if any journalists decided to come along), was still the principal mode of transport, and they were hardly placing *prima donna* demands when they stated a preference for 'hotels with showers.'

But part of it *was* glamorous too. How could there be a down side to *Kerrang*'s report of the three brothers at a star-studded A-list Status Quo party, which included Brian May, Lemmy, Brian Robertson, John Entwistle, Rick Wakeman and Phil Taylor? In the company of such musicians they were awestruck and Pat was more than happy to accept 'a kick up the arse' in constructive criticism about the music from people with such a pedigree. Hanging around with groveling would-bes, or trying to impress the right people and be seen at the right places, however was never going to be their scene. Pat told the papers that he was happy just to split after a gig and to give most of the parties a skip, reiterating 'I'm not in it for the wealth, or the prestige, or the honor of playing on stage. I regard myself as no different from anybody else. I just play a bit of music, that's all.' That had not changed from day one and in that there was complete harmony between the three brothers.

If the next port of call was destined to satisfy fully their desire to travel it was simultaneously going to challenge their desire to live a quiet life. Nobody could hope for that on the road in the USA with Ratt and Twisted Sister. Jive had bartered hard with Arista to get Mama's Boys out there and so Pat recalls with gratitude, and some bemusement, 'we got a release in America which was unheard of.' Three sold out nights at the Marquee (June 26th, 27th and 28th 1984) gave them the final warm up they needed before crossing the Atlantic and left a stunned Chris Welch certain that they were absolutely ready. Reviewing one of the performances for *Kerrang* he opened with the words 'Mama we're all stone deaf now', having been blown away by, as well as everything else, the ear-splitting volume. In his quest for sanctuary he had even stuck his head into the PA and found, to his surprise, that it was perhaps the quietest place in the building. He wrestled too with John's Irish brogue thinking *Power and Passion* was called *Parrot Fashion* and that the opener was *Gentlemen Roads* (instead of *Gentlemen Rogues*). In any case he concluded that it was a great gig and that no-one had left the sweat pit disappointed. Though Noddy Holder of Slade, who had originally penned *Mama We're All Crazee Now*, turned up and rumors abounded of a jam, Holder overdid the drink a bit and (in John's words) 'couldn't get onto the stage.' Backstage the brothers also caught the eye of a youthful Lars Ulrich. Tommy, far from being a reclusive or shy person

Peter Kerr and Pat in the USA: 'Gee, you guys did an awful amount of travelling. He didn't know about the other 10,000 the car had done.'

We are the road crew: Paul McGlue, Adrian Duffy and Peter Kerr.

A glamorous life on the road: [The crew were] 'smoking cigarettes, and would only look out for a few minutes each day then go back in again. That's why they were so white.'

Pat does his laundry on the road somewhere in America.

himself, commented that the Scandinavian 'would talk the hind legs off a donkey' and finished up, head in hands, with 'God! That boy can talk. '

As a final preparation for America, and in case *Mama We're All Crazee Now* didn't quite do it in the States (or in case it worked brilliantly well and needed to be followed up immediately) Mama's Boys recorded their next video *If The Kids Are United* at Queen Mary College, London. Indeed, Pat told the press that the next album was pretty much written too and could be tackled in earnest back in The Shed once the US tour was over. Cathal Dervan sent them on their way in an article called 'Mama's Boys Come of Age' pointing out that even as the reader was leafing through this article the boys would have already played to well over 200,000 people in the USA and would just be taking the stage in Houston in front of 80,000 more. The big time, he proclaimed, had arrived.

On the eve of their departure *Mama's Boys* was released and with it the long-awaited and expensive single / video, *Mama We're All Crazee Now* which immediately went into the US charts. Entirely coincidentally Quiet Riot, who had so successfully used Slade's *Cum on Feel the Noize* in 1983, had also planned to release *Mama We're All Crazee Now* as their follow up, presumably hoping for the same degree of commercial success second time round. When Quiet Riot singer Kevin du Brow heard that some other band had beaten them to it he went on the radio in America taking about 'the audacity of this Irish band. ' John was surprised as 'we didn't know Quiet Riot, we didn't know *Cum on Feel the Noize* -we barely knew *Mama We're All Crazee Now.* ' He could however see the marketing value in 'all this exposure mainly through Kevin's mouth' and felt certain that they were not at risk. After all, hadn't du Brow told the press clearly that Quiet Riot would never do another cover version, let alone another Slade song, so soon after *Cum on Feel the Noize*? Additionally, they came across as rather serious rock stars in the Los Angeles mode while Mama's Boys seemed capable of making fun of themselves. Their video certainly focused on this showing the band playing upstairs in a backstreet house in front of an impossibly large audience, with a Hilda Ogden style 'mum' terminating the performance by tweaking John's ear and telling him to get home for his tea which was stuck to the plate. The humor didn't mask the musicianship though and when US radio stations throughout 30 states started playing the two versions back to back (in some cases accompanied by the Slade original), then asking their listeners to call and state their preference, the results were overwhelmingly in favor of the Irishmen. In one case they got 99% of the total votes cast. Jive, it seems, had been correct all along. Though it had been tough to give up the Scorpions tour this was already paying dividends with up to eight showings of the

Mama's Boys with Rickey Medlocke (Blackfoot): 'They had lived for that moment. They were hungry for it.'

Pat and John with Jackson Spires (Blackfoot): 'Jackson [Spires] and I watched them from side-stage and we were floored.'

video a day on MTV. The door had been wedged well-and-truly open and Pat conceded the strategic value of the management decision even if he felt the choice of song was still a bit suspect

> Oh it worked big time. They were correct, absolutely 100% on the button. Because they believed in it, they pulled out all the stops. If they had believed in *Needle in the Groove* or *Runaway Dreams* it could have worked as well. They had one route, MTV, and that was the route they were going to go. We weren't going to rock the boat.

Given a moment or two to look around downtown Manhattan and to soak in the reality that the dream from the Derrylin farmhouse was actually coming true, Pat marveled 'You know this time last year we were playing gigs in Navan and Drogheda.'

The American tour started off in New York City on July 15th 1984 with a one-off support slot to Pat Travers / Jack Bruce at The Winery. Reports of the gig soon filtered back to Ireland and suggested rather oddly that Travers had tried to get them thrown off the stage after only 20 minutes of their set. Far from terminating their performance early and disappearing obediently however the brothers had gone back for an encore further irritating Travers who now pulled down the faders on the mixing desk. John Campion, an electrician from Cork whose sense of fair play was outraged by this act of sabotage, retaliated by rigging the electronics with a weak fuse so that when Pat Travers hit the first power chord of his own set it brought down the stage lights and blew everything else. Campion, on seeing the fruits of his labors, dashed out to the waiting car and shouted 'Go go go' as the crew sped off into the night with justice re-throned. John concludes 'It is just as well we were only doing one show with Pat Travers.' Soon after, Campion left the tour and went on to work with Prince and an array of other notables.

Next it was time to pick up on the Heavy Metal Massacre Tour at the Rochester Auditorium with Ratt (who had just released *Round and Round*) and Twisted Sister who needed no introduction at all. These were the up-and-comers. Ratt, with the pretty boy good looks of Steven Pearcy and the guitar wizardry of Warren de Martini, and Twisted Sister with the OTT attitude and made-up appearance of Dee Snider and his gang, made for an irresistible touring summer programme. Ratt were drug users, libido-led party animals hot off the Sunset Strip and dripping with attitude, while Twisted Sister were notoriously aggressive, ugly and the ultimate in foul mouthed rebel rock speaking for a bored and abused generation of kids who, in Dee Snider's words, were 'not gonna take it.' Teaming the unassuming and musically gifted Mama's Boys up with either, let alone both, was always going to be a newsworthy and absolutely dysfunctional marriage. Pragmatically however it made good business sense. Pat remembers: 'Ratt were good for 10,000 people, Twisted Sister were good for another 5000 or 6000, and Mama's Boys 2500 or 3000. ' Together they could sell out every show. John also observed this novel mix-and-match approach to marketing and saw a whole different attitude to concert going in general in the US that he had never seen before in the UK or Europe.

> You couldn't get away with that here at all. But in America, the people who go to see Duran Duran also go to see Ratt and Bon Jovi. In the UK it is all the long hair, the leather jacket with the arse of the trousers all ripped … metal fans. But in America it is a different experience. Neatly dressed and just out for the whole evening. The first time the lights went down and we went on, people were cheering and we were asking 'Why? You don't even know who we are or what we sound like yet. ' In the UK as the support you often play to half empty theatres as they are all out in the foyer drinking. They wouldn't shift their arses to come in and watch the support band. That's why I loved touring in America. You are not competing against the bar.

But some things never change and far from being swept along by the allure of cocaine, limos and penthouse suites, the boys opted for a rented car, a Ryder Truck (a sweat box with a hammock slung in the back) and the Motel 6 chain. For a very reasonable $39. 98 a night they could book two rooms and in so doing accommodate four people. Everyone else kipped in the van. Road manager Damian McCollum's remembers that sometimes the crew didn't get out of the back of the van for days at a time and were locked away in a troglodyte existence. He recalled they were content though, 'smoking cigarettes, and would only look out for a few minutes each day then go back in again. That's why they were so white. ' Damian had set all of this up in advance having been sent out to Arista's office in New York a week early. With a working tour budget of about $50,000 the name of the game was to stay on the road as long as possible. He watched A Flock of Seagulls come into the same office, pick up their cheque for the same amount, then blow it all in two and half weeks living like stars. Damian was having none of that and even got big bags of quarters collected for laundry and nightly phone calls home. In the days before mobiles, and with hotel phones costing what they did, the boys would manage in a phone box like anybody else. And as for Manhattan, Damian remembers

Tommy: 'Sure what are we all anyway except a bunch of auld musicians out on the road, playing a few tunes here and there.'

What in the name of Jaysus would you do in there? We'd come in and do interviews and anything they wanted during the days, then head out again to the Holiday Inn in Newark. It was all hectic and mad and expensive too.

Even this frugal existence got pricey after a while though and so the mile-ometers on the vehicles had to be disconnected so that the rental companies didn't know that they had been half way round America in the previous few weeks. The first 1000 miles were normally free so when the dial got up to 999 the meter would suddenly, and mysteriously, stop working. Even then Pat remembers how the car rental representatives would mop their brows and say "Gee, you guys did an awful amount of travelling." He didn't know about the other 10,000 the car had done.' On nights off from the main tour Damian booked the boys into a club here and a bar there to 'make a few quid.' Winding their way south towards Texas, Arizona, New Mexico and across to California, the McManus brothers continued to fill in the gaps in their timetable. Often this could be fairly out of the way, but they still managed to hook up again with Ratt, Twisted Sister and in some cases Fastway or Blackfoot, in time for the next stadium show. Whatever it took to stay out on the road for as long as was conceivably possible they would do, even if it meant playing every single night and driving non-stop through parched landscapes in a rented car and baking heat to do so. This is what it had all been for and now it was exceeding all expectations even if in 'Fast' Eddie Clarke's opinion 'They were living in the van, they were always in it. It was tough as fuck for them.' Rickey Medlocke could also see that the Irish brothers 'had lived for that moment. They were hungry for it.' Musically both Clarke and Medlocke were impressed too, the former saying 'They were a talented band man, absolutely cooking. I was heavily impressed;' the latter remembering 'Jackson [Spires] and I watched them from side-stage and we were floored.' This, the Blackfoot front man felt, was a band which 'shared common ground with [them through] the blues: two soulful bands very much enriched by feel.' Also, as Blackfoot were 'clean' at this stage (following a very heavy outing with Def Leppard) they found it 'really refreshing' to see a band coming from Europe which was 'straight as an arrow.'

After Reading and Dalymount, Twisted Sister's singer Dee Snider in particular was glad to welcome the boys onto his turf for a change. John remembers that 'Every single show after the opening number *Stay Hungry* he would talk about these sick Irish mother fuckers.' Pat remembers the same thing and acknowledges that 'Twisted Sister were fantastic to us.' Dee's banter from the stage would go

We are all sick mother fuckers. But you know who the sickest mother fuckers of all are? This band that was on before us. They are *driving around in a car.* So let's hear it for the sickest mother fuckers here tonight.

Damian also remembers Twisted Sister's unstinting support and their pleasant overall demeanor saying 'they were very laid back lads. ' In fact when the veneer was stripped away, Twisted Sister's rider, far from asking for cocaine and strippers stipulated a preference for lemon cake and tea. They had already been going for eleven years to attain this hard-fought-for success and weren't going to risk it now. Ironically then, despite appearances to the contrary, they had plenty in common with the Irish brothers who would also clean out the riders from the dressing rooms to live on. All the sodas, food, snacks and so on got crammed into a cooler box and taken back to the motel when the show was done. Outside their rooms they would then fire up a bar-b-q, get the instruments out and get going again with an impromptu trad session, joined by an array of truckers and passers by who were invited to join in. When money got even tighter they would order pizzas to be delivered to the wrong room number in the motel. The roadies would answer the door, say they knew nothing about it, and so the delivery guy would leave again. By the time he had found the right room (assuming that it was his mistake all along) the pizza was free, having taken more than 20 minutes to deliver. Tepid, stodgy pizza was hardly a gourmet diet, but it was economical.

Ratt on the other hand had only been going about eighteen months and were already huge. Their attitude, Pat recalls, was 'party stations. Go go go go!' Stephen Pearcy 'was one of those guys who would arrive with the coat over his shoulders, walk past you and not even see you. He was very much the star, you expect that of lead singers, they have to have an ego. ' But whereas in Damian's opinion Twister Sister were 'dreadful musicians', no-one could say that about Ratt. Perhaps it was contrasts like these that captured the imagination of the press who consistently spared time and column inches to search out and understand the less conspicuous McManus boys. Investigative journalism resulted in articles with titles such as 'Mama's Boys: Heavy Celtic Folk Rock' which then admiringly reported 'an intensity laced with the ethnic influences of our folk days. ' In contrast to their touring partners they seemed to exude ideas of loyalty, being a traveling band of gypsies where even the road crew had been with them since the beginning, and having parents who had supported them and had helped them right from the start. This was a long way from Twisted Sister's parent / authority hating *I am, I'm me* and from Ratt's legendary on-the-road antics. And yet, however different, all three bands seemed to hold each other in great esteem and even swapped tips and advice. In particular John remembers

> We got on extremely well with Robbin Crosby. He was an absolute gentleman, the boss of the band. It was his band. And he brought us back for the second tour again. They were good lads and they were some of the best memories we'll ever have.

Warren de Martini remembers the immediate chemistry too

> From the moment Robbin Crosby and me met Pat, John and Tommy McManus, we took to 'em, and from then on it seemed like we had always known them. I remember their fantastic energy and contagious good mood. I always got a 'wind-at-your-back' kind of feeling around them and it was easy to pick up on the wisdom they radiated. Maybe that came from growing up in Northern Ireland a few yards from the border, maybe it didn't. Never asked. Never will.

Pat remembers also that there was much to learn musically from Robbin Crosby and Warren de Martini, and that they had shown an interest in him too.

> It was a mutual admiration. We got on really well with Ratt, and they'd always be asking us 'How do you get that British sound?' And we would be there snooping round the back of the amps trying to see how they got that American sound. Warren de Martini was a phenomenal player. I would have no qualms about walking up to him and saying 'Jesus, I really loved that. How are you doing that?' 9 times out of 10 they would show you. '

He also attributes much of this camaraderie to Tommy who had confidence, not shared by his two older brothers, harnessed to a philosophy of 'If they don't want me in their band room it's no skin off my nose. ' He had done it in Los Angeles where he had spotted Jon Lord and been 'straight in there', with Ricky Medlocke of Blackfoot and Lynyrd Skynyrd, Noddy Holder of Slade, Steven Pearcy of Ratt ... the list goes on. Pat remembers

> He'd chat away to them all, road crews and everyone, calling them by their first names, and in return they would say after gigs 'Tommy, where are we off to tonight?' He would not be intimidated by them,

saying 'Ah sure they're great lads, a bit of fun. ' He just didn't care, maybe because of all that he had been through. Remember he was very young, he wasn't afraid of anyone. He'd just bound in there and shake hands. There were no airs and graces about him at all. Especially the guys from Ratt and big Robbin . . . hugging each other and planning a few places for after the shows. He would bring them all down to earth too saying 'Sure what are we all anyway except a bunch of auld musicians out on the road, playing a few tunes here and there. '

Any rivalry that did exist between Ratt and Mama's Boys was good natured and easy to handle. Bob Ashenmacher observed this keenly when he reported that the 'Warm-up trio easily steals Ratt's show' at Duluth Arena. Here Mama's Boys had literally startled the 2, 500 crowd who had come for the lip stick and glam of the Californians and instead been blown away not just by 'top of the neck screeching' but 'delicious' guitar playing in the vein of Roger Waters. In the end the reporter recalled Steven Pearcy shouting to the side stage 'Come on boys get your asses out here. '

Naturally drugs were everywhere and Robbin Crosby admitted 'Man we are selling a lot of records and we are making a lot of money, but right now we are shoving it all up our noses. ' In time, it would cost him his life. Mama's Boys kept well away from all of that and John remembers his bewilderment saying 'I've never felt the need to look for anything else as I was getting everything I wanted out of the music and being in a band. ' Pat also talked about the excesses saying

> We were aware of the other side but we chose not to go down that road. We could have, there were so many substances going about, but it just wasn't for us. We stayed away from the hotels and all the rest of it. We just weren't interested. We would just entertain ourselves. We were dead scared.

That said, the three brothers were front row observers to this party phenomenon and being human didn't object when Wally (the Ratt party organizer) invited them all back to the hotel from time to time to join in the shenanigans. John reminisces that the home grown image didn't always prevail and that

> the hotels that you'd be going back to with Ratt or Twisted Sister would always be swarming with police outside. We'd go back with them and just wreck the place. We'd skin up joints the size of an ice

cream cone in the lobby of the hotel. I remember Warren de Martini from Ratt grabbing it and saying 'Hey man, have you seen this? You gotta take a photograph of me with this thing.' And then the crew would get up and jump from table to table, spilling over drinks, and just being silly. Or doing what you are supposed to. The police were so busy holding back the crowds at the entrance to the hotel they couldn't see what was happening right behind them in the lobby.

A party in America: 'The police were so busy holding back the crowds at the entrance to the hotel they couldn't see what was happening right behind them in the lobby.'

Damian (who Pat calls 'the great leveller') was right there next to the McManus boys, keeping an eye on them, and warning them that should any of them think that they too might head in that direction they would be met with his simple motto: 'fuck that diva shite.' Meanwhile he looked in amazement at Wally's job description and remembers feeling that it was 'money for nothing that. There was money being fired out left right and centre and we were wondering had we enough fuel to get to the next city.' Fundamentally the brothers were just musicians wandering around playing music as they had always done, and as their parents had always done before them. Far from feeling like rock stars and getting inflated egos from the stadium gigs and all the adulation that comes with them, Pat remembers

It was no different to playing a trad[itional] session at home. We couldn't be something we were not. Maybe it would have been better

Pat and the fighting Irish: 'An impressed Tommy Lee said of the commotion surrounding Mama's Boys "Wow! FBI! Duuuuuudes!!!!! You rock. "'

Pushing the Synth-axe to its limits: 'A menacing attack. '

if we had come from the back streets of Belfast with a real chip on our shoulders, but we didn't. We weren't angry. We were having a great time.

While the LA caché was transient, ephemeral, and ultimately skin deep, what Mama's Boys was offering was permanent and inimitable. Dante Bonutto, author of *Mötley Crüe: The Official Biography (The First Five Years)*, saw this mutual, yet polar, attraction as no real surprise, and remembers

This was theatre. A sense of occasion. Britain was a little black and white as opposed to the technicolour west coast scene. But, if it was colour you were looking for you could get it musically from Mama's Boys. Visually, jeans and t-shirts, but musically more than that. Mama's Boys' *raison d'etre* was the music, not the lifestyle. It will become the subject for connoisseurs in the future. These are musicians, not entertainers.

One notable incident that did occur was when Tommy agreed to give two girls a ride to the next gig not knowing that it was illegal to carry people from one state to another, especially when one was on probation. When they got to their destination, John recalls, 'that was the last we saw of them' as they were clearly using the support band to get to the main act. After the gig was over the girls found their way onto the Fastway bus which then headed off to the next show with them on board. When the Fastway crew found out about all of the legal stuff, in Damian's recollections, they 'turfed them off the bus in the middle of the Nevada desert.' This led to a number of allegations about the legality of the girls' movements and also their welfare, which in turn led to an FBI raid on those who had perpetrated the crime. It all came to a head in San Diego when Mama's Boys were in the back stage area and the guys from Ratt were hanging out with Nikki Sixx and Tommy Lee from Mötley Crüe. John remembers

the next thing the FBI came screaming up to our trailer and took us out and started to take mug shots. All the guys from Mötley Crüe were watching these three young Irish lads as if to say 'You're fucking up our gig here dude.'

Warren de Martini of Ratt also remembers the incident

We were shooting the video footage for the song called *You Think You're Tough*. Lots of friends backstage: Carmine Appice, Jake E. Lee,

Live in France: 'Pat is, at the moment, a better guitarist than Michael Schenker.'

Tommy Lee. I remember Pat telling me that an impressed Tommy Lee said of the commotion surrounding Mama's Boys 'Wow! FBI! Duuuuuudes!!!!! You rock.'

'Fast' Eddie from Motörhead was less impressed. Not really caring too much about 'the young birds nicking stuff from our dressing room' he was certainly concerned when the law turned up. With the cat firmly among the pigeons, he recalls, 'We were freaking man.' Damian, pragmatic as ever, saw the commotion from a distance 'so I just kept on walking, and let Joe Wynne do the talking. The boys went on the stage shaking.' It all got patched up when the parents of the girls came to the show in San Diego, met the bands and heard that it had all been an innocent mistake after all. After the brief flirt with disaster however the new rule was 'no people on the bus.'

Another opportunity, a veritable once-in-a-lifetime chance to meet childhood heroes, presented itself when they finally got to *play with* Rush. John describes his devotion to the Canadian three-piece as nothing short of 'A ridiculous addiction' and remembers the 'we're-not-worthy' moment when they finally came face to face.

> When we walked into the arena Rush were doing the sound check and it actually sounded like the album, they were so perfect. Then Geddy Lee says 'OK guys, that's a wrap. Let Mama's Boys get their gear on.' We were like 'Fuck me! They've heard of us.' We just couldn't believe it. I'd go to get a coffee deliberately because I knew that Geddy, Alex and Neil were playing baseball back stage. And they'd talk to you! It was just an awesome trip, meeting your heroes and having the privilege of playing with them. We were like the guys from Wayne's World.

Pat's memories are the same 'They were quite brilliant, and humble, guys. They had nothing to prove to anyone. We were sitting with our mouths hanging open watching the sound check.' At concerts such as these pulling out the fiddle helped as Rush fans were real music lovers, not just rockers. Versatility and sheer musicianship were aces that Mama's Boys could play when the chips were down, and which had come in handy when they had shared a stage with the Stray Cats on a day off from the Ratt and Twisted Tour. Seeing 40,000 Teds reacting coldly to the opener *Gentlemen Rogues*, led to the immediate realization that this was the wrong band and the wrong place … until the fiddle came out. Pat remembers 'I think we kept that going for about 20 minutes.' John recalled that on another similar

Close Encounters: The new Synth-axe.

occasion when playing with Marie Wilson in Toulouse, France, the violin had dug them out of yet another hole.

Before they turned for home there was just time to squeeze in a quick visit to Canada with Ratt and Lee Aaron and / or Lita Ford, traversing the country through Montreal, Edmonton, Quebec and Toronto. This, it turned out, was another eye opener as on the one hand they would be playing in out-of-the-way strip clubs and trying to get the gear set up while the previous 'entertainment' was still in full swing, and on the other they were in bible bashing venues where John remembers that it was 'Like trying to draw blood from a stone. You just couldn't get them going. ' He never forgot though that 'When you've gone through the Hawkwind experience of people gobbing and throwing matches at you every night you can handle just about anything. '

Mama's Boys had proved that they could certainly compete with the best of American rock even if, as they told Robbi Millar from *Sounds*, the whole rock n' roll lifestyle was not for them. Pat derailed one interviewer from the outset of an interview with a warning that 'I can't talk about my big times or my new Porsche or my new girlfriend, 'cos I haven't got one. ' Millar didn't really need to be told that and observed 'It isn't easy to imagine him propping up the bar in some flashy New York niterie, bottle of Remy in one hand, trio of scatter-brained blondes in the other. ' Pat puts the reason beyond any doubt

> We were not inner city kids, and had nothing to be angry about and this was a vital, missing, ingredient. If we'd been in Birmingham or Manchester we'd have been a really tip top band because we would have had all that street cred and angst about inner city living, or whatever it is that happens to these guys. But we didn't. As much as we tried to do it, there was a kind of a phony element about it. We came from a farm with bales of hay, running around in fields in the summer time.

Though *Hit Parader* compared them to other famous rock brothers, like the Schenkers and the Youngs, it was becoming very clear for all to see that these were far-from-typical rock stars. Pat remembers the dichotomy saying the 'whole hair brigade was pure theatre. We were in show business. It was entertainment. We thought of ourselves as artists, we never thought that we had to be entertainers as well. ' When he was interviewed he was quick to emphasize this, reiterating 'I couldn't honestly see myself in chains and leather gear ripped up all over the place. ' Instead he reminded America 'You have to take us as we are. '

MAMA'S BOYS

DEEP PURPLE
ROCK GODDESS
BRYAN ADAMS
URIAH HEEP
ATTENTAT ROCK

M 1523 - 9 - 15 F
Mensuel 15 FF - Belgique 116 FB

John on the front cover of Hard Rock Magazine: 'The juxtaposition of dreams and reality.'

Chapter 4: 'Good Afternoon Knebworth'

The American jaunt completed, every last dime of the tour money spent, and now in London again, there was little time to waste and no time at all to recover. Ever mindful of the progress which had been made, and nervous about losing such hard-fought-for momentum, Jive got them back into Battery Studios with Chris Tsangerides to start recording *Power and Passion*. Liberated from the restraints of the previous record and free now to nurture new tunes and styles, the legendary Cypriot producer immediately advised the boys to widen the repertoire of instruments to cover what they could actually offer. Rather than following a prescribed rock n' roll route that could so easily be imitated or replicated, why not show off their uniquely diverse musical parameters which would surely be the envy of so many other bands? When you have the natural advantage, he argued, use it. This had also been Joe Wynne's advice when he had recommended 'Stay with what you know. You are Irish, you are musical and you are not angry, so don't be anything else.' And so within a few days the uilleann pipes, the fiddle, and a host of other character building assets arrived into the studio to add, what Tsangerides called, the 'history, story telling, identity, color, flavor, and stamp of Mama's Boys.' Everything except the kitchen sink it seemed went onto *Power and Passion*. And it worked. From the minute snippets and clips were leaked it was obvious that the critics were going to love it. At *Kerrang*, for example, a pre-release cassette provoked a reviewer to suggest that this approach would 'shake the foundations of the rock hierarchy' before unreservedly declaring that 'an album destined to become a rock classic' was on its way. From such a specialist magazine this was high praise indeed, and true to their word, when Geoff Banks reviewed the album in its entirety, it got a perfect 5 Ks (which means 'Kolossal', with I K being 'Kompost'). He declared enthusiastically that the opus 'had more power than a runaway cruise missile and more passion than a U2 world tour.' If anything, he argued, the word 'class' should have been added to the title of the LP in order to do full justice to a band that was no longer a rising force but now a mature and confident world class act. According to Banks it had it all: 'rabble rousing stompability', more than one 'football terrace chorus', singing which lunged 'head first into the danger zone', and an unrelenting 'menacing attack' on drums. The instrumental, *The Professor II* (using the state of the art Roland Synth-axe) was also a welcome

MAMA'S BOYS (from left):
John McManus, Pat McManus
and Tommy McManus

Pic Ray Palmer

Ray Palmer's photo shoot: 'Unfortunately a lot of people judge a book by its cover.'

addition, with Tommy and Pat jousting with mesmerizing agility to remind the fans of what they had seen / were missing at the gigs. It was these very fans who knew that not everything could, or should, be packaged up into a three minute song. Why not enjoy pure musicianship even if, in terms of radio play and single sales, it was something close to commercial suicide? *Run,* or *Let's Get High,* on the other hand could easily go to the top of the charts were they released as singles. In fact the entire album went to No 1 in the *Hard Top* magazine in France, ahead of Accept, Deep Purple, Foreigner and Ratt, while *Hard Rock* magazine put John on the front cover. In the UK *Sounds* saw it enter their charts at No 2 and in the USA the LP dug itself in for a total of 14 weeks in Billboard.

But it was not all plain sailing and some hard core fans were wondering why they had been dished up *Straight Forward* and *Needle in the Groove* yet again. Though seventeen original tracks had been laid down for the album Jive made the final selection to include the live classic (the former) and one last shot at that illusive hit single (the latter). How many times would the fans take the same revamped songs appearing every time a record was released, especially when they were being deprived of brand new songs that had already been recorded? Would they ever see the light of day? The old songs were now just that ... old songs. It was unlikely that any new rearrangement or re-recording of a dated tune was going to break them if it hadn't already done so. But Jive kept trying. Pat now sees this as a mistake and says 'Maybe we should have said "No, it is fine the way it is". ' He also remembers wondering, if a minor modification to *Needle in the Groove* had failed to get them the hit they needed, what might the record company ask them to do next? Thankfully not everyone saw it this way and Geoff Banks actually commended Jive's decision, concluding that the old tunes had finally been given the thorough 'seeing to' that they had always needed. The cover of the LP was another sore point boasting as it did another semi-clad woman clawing at Pat's Flying V, reclining on a throne in an Ozzy-style studio set. While this was not unusual in 80s rock it nevertheless came across as puerile and in no way representative or relevant to the band in question. John remarked that it actually damaged sales instead of enhancing them as 'Unfortunately a lot of people judge a book by its cover. ' But it wasn't just a matter of aesthetics or even taste. At the height of the Tipper Gore sponsored P. M. R. C. (Parents Music Resource Center) activities in the USA, shops wouldn't even stock the album with that image and so what resulted was even worse, ie a photo of the three boys, minus the model, sitting on the same throne. From predictably offensive rock kitsch it had

Live in Lille, France, 1984: Ready to 'shake the foundations of the rock hierarchy.'

Live in France, 1984: 'A veritable hot house[s] of sardine-packed euphoria.'

Pat tunes up back stage in America: 'We thought the sky was the limit. We thought it would go on forever.'

John with Jon Bon Jovi: 'When they went on the reaction they got was just ridiculous, like Beatlemania. Not even Ratt who were headlining came anywhere close. It was obvious that something massive was going to happen.'

become instantly forgettable in a market that desperately needed image to sell. A glance at Mötley Crüe, Ratt or Poison and their imaged-based helter skelter successes, would tell even an outsider to the industry that. Years later Pat told *Hot Press* 'We were absolutely mad when that sleeve came out. We hadn't wanted that at all. ' Why were they being marketed as misogynistic affiliates of the LA scene? To recap -their debut album was on Pussy Records, *Turn it up* had had a topless rock-chick on it, and now there was this banned cover. Worse was to follow when Ray Palmer did a photo shoot of the three brothers, sticking rigidly to cliché and formula, and making them peer uncomfortably through a pair of stocking-ed legs. This was not what Mama's Boys wanted to be; it was what they were told they ought to be in order to sell. Worst of all, the music was beginning to suffer too. All other peripheral considerations could have been overlooked so long as the music had been allowed to be written and performed in all its genuine and talented complexity -but it was not. Pat was struggling, writing songs on the road at 2. 00am in the morning 'to order. ' How could anyone produce good work knowing that an album a year was expected whether it had been created or not? The spontaneity of The Shed, the feedback and interaction of the brothers, and the trial and error live, was all being replaced with a need to produce right on schedule, to look and to sound a certain way. What they had done, and been, up to and including Reading had been pure, unsupported, down to earth Mama's Boys, and that is what had been signed. Now, whereas the Advances were nice and being an 'insider' in the music industry a great boost, success was coming at a horrific price artistically. The boys were beginning to wonder where the carefree gigging had gone to. John looks back with a healthy dose of cynicism and sighs 'You are working for a corporation now. They didn't understand what they had signed. ' In an interview with Derek Oliver Pat shared his growing concerns saying

> It's not like the early days anymore where nobody cared if something didn't go according to plan. In those days we used to laugh it off. Now we wake up with heavy responsibilities: five or six road crew, a manager, stacks of gear, a record company running around us talking money, big money … For guys who just want to play music it all seems a bit over the top.

Though sympathetic, Oliver mulled this over and concluded that if anyone was going to join Zeppelin and Purple (and he said they could) they would have to remain at their creative best whatever the circumstances. Pat rounded up the tense interview saying how deeply felt it had all become.

John and Adrian Duffy on the road in America

Peter getting cleaned up

Paul backstage in America

It is hard to get back to reality. You begin to question the whole thing, like, 'Am I really worth anything? Is it really happening and am I conning people left, right and centre?' You become a little paranoid.

In a business where everyone was cock sure, outgoing and self confident, Pat spoke for himself and his brothers when he concluded 'I don't feel myself with them at all. That whole star trip doesn't appeal to us at all. ' Today he sums it up in a few words, saying that his had become 'a dog's life. '

When *Power and Passion* was finished and released, it was time to get back out on the road again in Ireland and the UK, backed up with the release of a new single *Hard n' Loud* and *Lettin' Go* (with a long version of *Without Your* live from San Antonio, Texas on the 12"). Mama's Boys could always be relied on live and once again proved that they warranted all the expectation and hype by delivering their finest shows to date. A bewildered Derek Oliver looked back on 'a veritable hot house[s] of sardine-packed euphoria pushing the temperatures way up to unbearable levels, even on the coldest nights. ' In Dublin, with Bernie Marsden's Alaska supporting, a breathless Mary Anne Hobbs finished her gig review with strong words and sentiments about what she had just witnessed, saying 'it only remains for me to confirm that the tricky trio are indeed living, breathing Irish history.' Sylvie Simmons of the *New Musical Express* then interviewed them for a major article called 'Real Mama's Boys' in which she professed deep musical, professional and personal respect for the brothers. She also reported that *Mama's Boys*, the album, had by now shifted a healthy 100,000 copies in the US and predicted that *Power and Passion* would go even further (by November it had topped 120,000). Aware of this, the specialized music journals dutifully queued up to re-tell the entire story of the rise and rise of the band: from the farm house in Derrylin to recently seeing themselves on the TV in New York; from the dance halls of Ireland to the high media profile tussling with Quiet Riot; from the stadiums of North America all the way back to proud parents who had actually bought them their PA and a four ton truck to start gigging with (even if, in John's words, 'we were crap at the time'). The story, like the music, was irresistible.

To capitalize on the moment it was decided that Mama's Boys should be sent back to the USA, this time to tour with Ratt and the up-and-coming Bon Jovi. The boys from Ratt they already knew and liked, and in the short time since their last tour with them in the states the Californians had gone through the roof in album sales, packed out stadium shows, and now adorned the cover of just about every major music magazine. Nevertheless they pushed hard to get the Irish brothers out with them again as Warren de Martini remembers 'For years afterwards, every time the topic of bands to tour with came up, Robbin would look at me and say in a whining voice "Can't we just get Mama's Boys?" and I'd double it "Yeah, can't we just … ?"' Pat remembers the pleasure of renewing his friendship with the guys from Ratt who, despite being very different, had always taken 'a shine to us because there were no airs and graces with us, we weren't trying to outplay them, or out glam them.' Robbin Crosby and Tommy rekindled their friendship too based on a shared, similar, and wicked sense of humor. Pat now remembers the late Ratt guitarist warmly, saying 'You couldn't meet a nicer guy than Robbin Crosby. A big, tall, gentle guy. A real nice bloke.'

Bon Jovi had not quite broken through yet though were certain to do so sometime in the coming months as MTV was pushing them hard. The blockbusters *Livin' on a Prayer* and *You Give Love a Bad Name* were only just around the corner but not yet in sight. Mama's Boys, it was felt, had the same potential and were sure, with Bon Jovi, to follow the success of Ratt. As Ratt was headlining, Bon Jovi and Mama's Boys took turns to open each show and also shared a band room where inevitably they became friends. Pat recalls that Richie Sambora was very human and respectful, and that Tico was the perfect southern gentleman. He also remembers 'It was very easy to see that they were going to be huge.' Jon Bon Jovi, John remembers, was already a superstar and knew his band was about to eclipse the Los Angeles upstarts entirely

> When they went on the reaction they got was just ridiculous, like Beatlemania. Not even Ratt who were headlining came anywhere close. It was obvious that something massive was going to happen. I'm not kidding. You couldn't hear anything with girls going fucking apeshit.

Within a year the prophecy had been fulfilled and the role had been reversed with Ratt supporting Bon Jovi on yet another marathon hike across the continent.

Touring in America all came down to marketability again, as it had done the previous year with Twisted Sister and Ratt. Now, however, the size of the venues was becoming enormous and, if anything, rather impersonal. The boys felt most comfortable with crowds of about 800 – 1500 where there was still some connection with the punters and therefore plenty of atmosphere. Pat had always vouched for this more up-close-and-personal approach remembering that he had once abandoned a Queen gig at the RDS in Dublin half way through to go see Dr Feelgood playing at the Olympia where 'the place was heaving.' Freddie Mercury cavorting around a gigantic stage with all his camp theatricality, to a stadium of adoring fans had failed to impress Pat. Instead, at the smaller venue

> There were four lights on either side of the stage and the boys just belted it out. That's where I want to be. Never mind sitting on Superman's shoulders – a load of old baloney.

But those days of club scale gigging for Mama's Boys looked like they belonged very firmly in the past and, like it or not, this was the way it was going to be from now on.

Wally, the Ratt party organizer, continued to build the McManus brothers into the after gig party schedule when possible, though as often as not the boys had to split early as they were driving themselves to the next city and the next show. Ratt, on the other hand, could party all the time and soon evidence of this began to creep into their work when they would miss sound checks and do error-ridden shows after particularly tough nights. It was clear that they had plenty of money but that they were losing it as quickly as they were making it, not least through the size of the cabaret they had taken out on the road. They had gone from playing small venues in LA, like the Rainbow and the Roxy, to having three levels of scaffolding in a stadium hauled around by four or five trucks and four or five tour buses. The bill for Holiday Inns for all of the crew and whoever else joined in every single night soon added up. The girls, the drink, the drugs, the excesses of Harley Davidsons and sports cars .... Ratt had it all. Meanwhile, stone cold sober and crammed into their trusty hire car, the McManus brothers were driving through the night to the next city and the Motel 6 which awaited them. Warren de Martini reflects on that magic of the tour which perhaps he did not appreciate fully enough at the time

> It was 1984: the 1969 of the 80s. Looking back it was kinda like riding a roller coaster for a year. It started playing clubs like the Whisky-A-Go-Go in LA, to L'Amour in Brooklyn and by mid-summer, to arenas. Mama's Boys joined up with Ratt as this tour hit full swing. Pat McManus tearing it up on guitar and then switching to fiddle, Johnny on bass and lead vocal, Tommy on the drum kit. We loved this band. We didn't realize it then but this was a major peak in all our lives – the juxtaposition of dreams and reality.

Though Mama's Boys were picking up 'a grand a night' on this tour, all expenses had to be covered and this left them with a *per diem* of $20. Fuelled by the success of the live shows *Power and Passion* was now shifting tens of thousands of copies in the US. Compared to Ratt's *Out of the Cellar*, however, which was closing in on the two million mark, sales were comparatively sluggish from a marketing executive's point of view. And so, even as they made their way along thousands of kilometers of highways, even as the shows were met with rapturous applause and critical acclaim, and even as merchandise flew off the stalls, the executives from Jive had started looking anew at the three piece and wondering what to do with it next.

Then came a dilemma: a nice one, but a dilemma nonetheless. Half way through the successful, and expensive, American tour Mama's Boys were offered a slot on the Knebworth Festival bill which would see them sharing a stage with Deep Purple, Meat Loaf, Scorpions, Blackfoot, UFO, Mountain and Alaska. As the festival was thousands of miles away in the UK, and as there were no real gaps in the US touring schedule in June, a pragmatist would have had difficulty in demonstrating that this was anything other than a financial own goal that would cripple the band. On the other hand how could anyone with a love of rock music turn down such an offer? Wasn't this the dream from The Shed finally coming true? The McManus brothers weren't going to miss this for the world whatever the accountants said, and so the decision to drop everything and go was immediate. John looks back on it and laughs 'Are you joking. It's Deep Purple. ' And so began the marathon trek from Oklahoma to New York to Heathrow to Knebworth, to play the most important 45 minute set of their lives. John's triumphant, long-drawn-out shout of 'Good Afternoon Knebworth' after the opener, *Gentleman Rogues*, conveyed only confidence, and nothing of fatigue or nerves. This was the reward for all those years of slogging and accordingly he remembers that on that stage 'We thought the sky was the limit. We thought it would go on forever. ' Pat also looks back on it as 'the pinnacle of that period in the band's history. '

Knebworth '85 was probably one of the rainiest festivals in UK history and to this day is remembered as 'Mudworth. ' Accordingly, the crowd of 80,000 soaked and filthy punters decided to occupy itself by throwing mud which at times became the principal form of entertainment. Roadie Paul McGlue, peering from the side stage out over the battlefield, warned John 'You are going to get destroyed if you go out there. Pat's backline is ruined.' Pat remembers a similar conversation when 'A roadie came in and said "It is mayhem out there. " He was actually frightened. They were flinging mud in all directions. It was all over the cabinets and everything. ' But, as with Reading in 1983, 'the minute we came out it stopped. ' In the eye of the storm the stage was theirs and well used. In fact they cranked up the volume so loud they actually blew a third of the PA, ruining Deep Purple's assault on The Who's 'loudest ever gig in Britain' crown which was due to be contested that day. When the last strains of the crowd sing-along in *Sha-na-na-na-na* had died away, and as soon as they had taken their final bow to the cheering Knebworth crowd, the mud flinging started again and 'Meat Loaf got pasted. ' Meanwhile they were already back on a plane to New York, then to Minneapolis, and later that night were on stage with Iron Maiden without so much as a break for a shower. Had it been worth it? You didn't need to ask! There was absolutely no doubt about it -the dream was coming true. In fact, the dream had just come true.

On the final night of the US tour before they went into Canada, Mama's Boys played to 15,000 rowdy punters in Seattle. During the last song, John remembers, the crowd seemed to get louder and louder, leading him to think 'Fuck me man, they are really digging this. ' Suspicious of the disproportionate level of enthusiasm he finally turned round to see what was going on behind him and saw the guys from Ratt and Bon Jovi on stage with them, egging the crowd on and encouraging them to sing *Straight Forward*. Every time John opened his mouth to lead, however, Robbin Crosby, already standing behind him and playing his bass, poured Jack Daniels down his throat and his front, which, for a teetotaler was off-putting to put it mildly. This symbolized their final acceptance into the fraternity of rock musicians in front of the fans who had been so convincingly won over. John allows himself a pat on the back saying 'We deserved to be on stages like that as things were going well for us at that time. '

The frantic pace continued and before long the brothers took to the stage with Sting, Foreigner, Rough Cutt and Dio in front of 80,000 people on the other side of the world at the Super Rock Festival in Japan. The festival itself was eventful from the very beginning. Firstly, John remembers seeing one of his heroes in an unusual light when

> This massive row broke out just outside our bus between Sting and the promoter. He had just sacked his whole band about 10 minutes before he was due to go and do his performance. Sting suggested that he would do an acoustic set alone but the promoter wasn't having any of it.

Pat takes up the story

> They had a row right outside our portacabin during which Jimmy Bain pushes the window open and says in a Glaswegian accent 'I'll play the bass for you, wee man. ' Sting just looked at him in disdain and walked away.

John Live in France, 1985: 'Man, they are really digging this.'

Pat Live in France, 1985: 'More power than a runaway cruise missile and more passion than a U2 world tour.'

Pat live on the road to Rouen, 1985.

Next, Mama's Boys' time slot was altered significantly so that by the time they took to the stage it had become so late at night that it was actually getting bright again. John recalls

> We actually went on after Foreigner. It was about 3. 30 in the morning. I remember going into Dio's band room and shouting at everyone to wake up as we were about to go on. Of course Vivian was there. We knew Vivian Campbell very well from back in the Sweet Savage days.

Lastly, John continues, 'I remember going out on the stage and every one was standing still, not much movement, and I was thinking "Shit!" Then you get to the end of the song and there just this unmerciful roar of approval and then it is back to silence again. ' It certainly seemed true that no two audiences were alike and certainly not in any two countries. The show finished with John stripped to the waist, dueling with Pat and aiming his bass out over an appreciative crowd, while Tommy worked himself up into a frenzy. John, having learned something from his apprenticeship in the USA, and now with earrings, sunglasses and backcombed hair complete, even made it onto the cover of a calendar in Japan with a photograph taken during this closing.

With no time to lose it was onto a plane again, to Europe this time, to tour with Gary Moore. Pat spoke enthusiastically to the press about how Horslips had always talked about their love of Germany and how, now, he too could not wait to go. Damian, ever pragmatic, and hardly likely to be swept away on a euphoric wave approached the tour with a modicum of well-guarded cynicism as

> Everybody told us Gary Moore would be a pain in the hole to work for, a real pain in the arse, but he was great with us. We always got a sound check and in a couple of shows in France he actually opened up for us.

Damian's ethos of 'nice gets you everywhere' was certainly a management technique that others in the rock and roll circus could have learned from. The music was good, the band becoming lucrative (or at least sustainable), and the ambition of touring the world and taking music to hundreds of thousands of people, almost completely realized.

In the midst of all the euphoria and the razzamataz however, the fact that Tommy was beginning to get more lethargic and had started to find

At the airport, heading for Japan

Local publicity shot in Japan: 'Pat McManus tearing it up on guitar and then switching to fiddle, Johnny on bass and lead vocal, Tommy on the drum kit. We loved this band.'

John messing around at the hotel

INTERVIEW WITH

SUPER ROCK '85 IN JAPAN

アメリカのコンサートは女の子だらけだネ!!

by Naomi Ohno / BURRN!

pix: Hiroyuki Yoshihama

インタビューア●大野奈菜美(本誌)

Ready to play (Photo by Hiroyuki Yoshihama): 'The tricky trio are indeed living, breathing Irish history.'

it very difficult to stay awake, had gone almost unnoticed. Even if anyone had spotted it, it would hardly have seemed unusual bearing in mind the exhausting schedule that he and his brothers were now on. In any case, he was hiding it as much as he could and fighting it mentally with all his determination as he probably knew, deep down, what this was likely to be. In retrospect, John remembers the slow, terrible, realization

> Tommy was constantly sleeping. Normally he wouldn't want to miss a single second on the road but in America he would wake up to go into a service station to get a coffee or whatever and then come back out to the car and go straight back to sleep. So we knew something was wrong. He was very lethargic all the time. You push it right to the back of your mind what it might be. But it never affected the performances.

John still has a photograph of Tommy spread out across the seats sleeping on the flight to Japan for the Super Rock '85 Festival in Tokyo. The photo now has a significance that it did not have at the time, cataloguing as it does the start of Tommy's descent back into serious illness. Every day it became more and more noticeable, at least harder and harder for him to hide, and soon it was clear that he would have to be re-hospitalized. The leukaemia was back and this time worse than before. Given his straight choice he would probably have played on and dismissed the disease with the contempt he believed it deserved, but reluctantly he took advice from those around him and let Jim de Grasso (a friend of Chris Tsangerides) temporarily take his drum stool. Pat told a journalist

> I can still remember exactly the moment the doctors told Tommy about this. Tommy was furious. Not because of his illness, but because of the European Tour that soon would take place. He told the doctors that surely he couldn't let his brothers down. He was furious.

At first John and Pat wanted to cancel the tour entirely, but they had contractual obligations and so de Grasso came to Fermanagh, rehearsed in The Shed for a week, then went out on the road having memorized the set perfectly (This tour, his first, was the start of a glittering career that would see him work with Y&T, Alice Cooper, Megadeth, Ozzy, White Lion and Dave Lee Roth). Though from the American school of rock n' roll, Jim got a sobering, nightly dose of Damian's Irish pragmatism to keep him on the

'Mama's Boys "Garnements"' French Magazine cover: *'We deserved to be on stages like that as things were going well for us at that time.'*

(Above) Pat live in Belfast: 'He [Tommy] convinced us that he would be fit to do Ireland. Both Pat and I told him not to think about the Irish tour, but he was adamant.'

(Left) John Live in France: 'The sheer amount of vocal work that John had to do every night was tough. He was having problems though. He needed a rest.'

right tracks. Damian recalls that the new recruit was

> A lovely fella but a bit posy and stuff. He had this thing about firing his drum sticks out into the crowd at the end of every show. I had to take him to one side and say, firstly, you are going to put someone's eye out doing that, and secondly, we can't afford them. Hold on to them. He came round to our way of thinking and got the sense of humor after a while.

In the meantime, and on a much more serious subject, John broke the silence and explained to a German magazine what was going on with Tommy.

> For all of us it was a blow, however not unexpected. The fact that Tommy has leukaemia was known to us ten years ago. But at that time, because of his age, he couldn't get the necessary very heavy therapy yet.

Pat told *Kerrang* a similar story but was quick to emphasize that this would have absolutely no impact on the future of the band

> This has been a terrifically difficult time for both the band and our family. At one point Tommy lost a lot of weight and was extremely ill. There's no question of him not continuing his career with the rest of us; the only difference will be that we'll have to look after him a bit more and that's no problem.

Phoning back to the hospital in Belfast every night became a part of the concert routine, and in return the vibe coming back through the telephone wires from Tommy was increasingly positive. Pat even remembered that Tommy had talked the doctors into letting him have a drum kit down in the cellar of the hospital where he kept practicing for when he was fit again (much to the annoyance of the other patients within ear-shot). Gary Moore also made sure that good-will messages got back frequently to keep his spirits up. But Tommy was missing out, and he knew it. There was no way he would be able to tolerate this situation for much longer.

Parting company with Moore after Germany, Mama's Boys made their way into France and through to the final date of their own headlining tour in Reims on December 17, 1985. By now the impatient Tommy had deemed himself sufficiently well to sign himself out of treatment and catch up with his brothers. Expertly concealing any lingering symptoms, and probably partially convinced of his own recovery, he insisted that Mama's Boys play a few Christmas concerts in Ireland. John remembers 'He convinced us that he would be fit to do Ireland. Both Pat and I told him not to think about the Irish tour, that everything was panning out fine with Jim, but he was adamant.' So when the time came John picked Tommy up in Derrylin and together they drove down to Limerick to meet up with the crew which was just coming back with the gear from mainland Europe. There was a problem however as the trucks coming in had got delayed at customs with the result that the show had to be pulled at the very last minute. John sighs 'I was secretly relieved as the venue had a low ceiling and I knew that the lights would be right beside Tommy's head which would be no good for him at all.' The two nights in Belfast, and two nights in Dublin, which followed would be in much larger venues and so pose much less of a threat to his health. Thinking about Tommy's performance in the capital cities John now reflects 'You would never in a million years believe that the guy had just come out of hospital having just had all this chemo', but then adds seriously 'he shouldn't have been doing it at all.' Though the performances had been flawless, and though the brothers and the fans had loved the return of Mama's Boys to their home shores in the original format, it was clear the triumph had come at a price when Tommy had to be rushed back to hospital immediately after the final show.

A proper break was evidently needed not only to get Tommy back on his feet but also to take stock of the roller coaster year that had been and to think about what to do next. Perhaps surprisingly some people close to the band were beginning to harbor doubts about what the future might bring. Chris Tsangerides, for example, noted with some trepidation that for all they were flying very high indeed it was not yet high enough to succeed in this industry. Poised so close to absolute success he knew that without a solid smash hit on the radio and on MTV, and a major headlining tour of the US, Mama's Boys might yet find themselves in trouble. It was precisely here the cracks began to show in terms of policy and marketing. Though he went along with all of their decisions at the time, John now reflects 'All Jive needed to do was make sure we got back into the studio, record a really good rock record, then get us back out on the road with Bon Jovi in America, or onto the festival scene. Forget the radio.' Pat agrees saying that it was time now to create the perfect album and back it up with the perfect tour. Instead, Jive insisted that a 3 minute, punchy, commercially digestible, single was needed, and this was the one thing Pat felt unable to deliver. Even today, concerning this 'write-to-order' mentality, he admits 'I can't do it. It's not that I don't like doing it, I can't do it. Believe me, if I could do it I'd be there as quick as lightning, but it wasn't my forté at all. ' Nonetheless, if Mama's Boys didn't come up with something fairly urgently they would have to take the consequences. In fact behind the scenes Jive had already begun to sketch out a Plan B that was as shocking as it was unthinkable to the legion of fans who had watched the rise of the band from the dance halls of Fermanagh to the legendary stage at Knebworth.

As the search for a single progressed, and in the inevitable period of inactivity brought about by Tommy's treatment, rumors began to circulate that John was having trouble with his voice. The demands of rock singing at a phenomenal volume and right at the top of his range (in his words 'so that only dogs could hear it'), was taking its toll. In the studio, and for the first few gigs of any tour, this high pitched style presented no problems at all, but after six months on the road he got the sinking feeling that he was letting down both Pat and Tommy. John remembers 'The first thing you do in the morning when you wake up is swallow to see how your throat is. And you didn't get any sympathy either, let me tell you that. ' Pat remembers 'The sheer amount of vocal work that John had to do every night was tough. He was having problems though. He needed a rest. The whole vocal thing fell on his shoulders. ' And so the press began to leak reports that, despite having performed perfectly throughout the recent tours and at Knebworth, a specialist who was with them in France had claimed that in his professional life he had rarely seen a worse case of strain. John, the alarmist reports continued, was ordered to stop singing immediately or face the very real prospect of losing his speaking voice too. Though there is a kernel of truth at the heart of this (in John's words 'part of that is true … but exaggerated slightly') the reality is that the record company wanted to change the three-piece formula and add a singer for commercial / marketing reasons. Manager, Michael Deeney, remembers the behind-the-scenes logic whereby John's voice was deemed to be 'very good, but it [was] not exceptional … and this is a very competitive business. ' The quest for the single, the need for radio play, and the possibility of an image change, required Mama's Boys to abandon their three-brother-status and become a four piece. This was going to be a gamble and one which John himself saw as a mixed blessing. On one hand 'When the idea was suggested to me ultimately I didn't put up any barriers whatsoever. I was happy to pass that responsibility on. ' On the other hand, it represented a loss of control for the band to the extent that a business decision could create such a radical shift away from the formula which had been working for all these years and up to this very point. Pat goes on to say

Looking back on it I wasn't happy with the way it ended up with John being in the role of just bass player. It wasn't right. We should have had enough balls, particularly me probably, to stand up and say it is not right to the record company. But it was the same old thing. We were too scared to rock the boat. We should have said would you ever get lost. But once again we just bit our tongues and got on with it, which we shouldn't have done.

With the benefit of hindsight (which is 20/20) John now laments the decision

Whatever it was they saw in Mama's Boys when they say is in 1983 on the stage at Reading and signed us, they should have continued to exploit, to realize that this is never going to be a radio friendly act. Never! You build up your following, and you become successful and you sell albums simply through the fan base you have built up ... and we were building up a huge fan base.

What had started out as three brothers working together in The Shed, was now being turned into something else. John bemoans their fate saying 'What happened is that we completely lost any identity that Mama's Boys ever had.' The Irish accent had gone, the singer and the hallmark style had 'been wiped off the face of the earth.' The ultimate lack of respect for their ability to make it on their own terms came when the owner of Jive sent *Addicted to Love* by Robert Palmer to Pat with the message 'This is number one in America. Can you write something like it?' John now appreciates that 'They are the moments when you write back and say 'Fuck off'! You want a band that plays and writes like Robert Palmer go and find one. This is not the band you signed at Reading. That's not what we are.' But they didn't say this nor did they protest at all and so Pat started writing alone. To make matters worse, the old formula for rehearsing had also been disrupted by circumstances beyond their control.

We couldn't play as a band because Tommy was ill. We would normally have gone out to The Shed, played with the ideas, thrashed it out like we normally did and then killed each other for the next three hours ... and that didn't happen because he was in the hospital.

An arduous and drawn-out search for just the right singer to fill John's shoes also got underway at this time. Dave King had been auditioned years ago and had come pretty close to fitting in, so the boys knew, at least in principle, that it should be possible to find a suitable front man. Before long

New singer Keith Murrell: 'The jewel in the crown.'

Drummer Tommy's tragic secret is out...
MAMA'S BOY IS BATTLING CANCER!

• Tommy McManus: "This is something I am going to have to live with."

The tragic secret of a young Irish rock star was revealed this week.

Tommy McManus, the 19-year-old drummer with Mama's Boys, is battling against the killer disease leukaemia.

He has been missing from the group for the past two months, during which time he's been undergoing intensive treatment at the Royal Hospital in Belfast.

When I contacted him at his Fermanagh home yesterday, Tommy told me that he's making good progress and hopes to be back in action soon.

Mama's Boys are starting an Irish tour next week and he hopes to join his brothers Pat and John.

The courageous young man said: "This is something I'm going to have to live with.

"I first got leukeamia when I was eight years old and was clear until recently.

"Doctors are pleased with my present progress, so I'm keeping my fingers crossed."

Press leaks of Tommy's illness: 'Only a miracle could have saved Tommy and we still can't believe that it happened.'

Rick Chase emerged as the frontrunner and actually moved to Derrylin to live and work with the band on what would become *Growing Up The Hard Way*. When they moved to Dublin to start recording however he suddenly seemed uncomfortable and soon was unable to record anything at all. Exasperated, John asked him 'Well what happens if you can't sing in Paris either? What are we going to do there?' Pat had not been one hundred percent satisfied stylistically either, remembering 'He wasn't exactly singing the songs the way we were hearing them in our head. He had a more theatrical style. We wanted more of a lonesome, dirty, low down, bluesy kind of voice. ' Pat recalls that the decision was taken out of their hands anyway when 'He really genuinely did develop throat problems. ' And so that was that. Rick left the band before he ever really got started.

Without a singer again, and with Tommy still hospitalized, the opportunity arose to play at the Milton Keynes Bowl with Status Quo, Jethro Tull, Rory Gallagher, Magnum and Nazareth. What's more, as a traveling festival, it was going to move on for two further shows in Germany (Dinkelsbuhl and Nurenburg) when England was done. This was too much for Tommy. There was no way on earth he was going to miss an opportunity like this, and so he checked himself out of hospital. The video footage of the performance at the subsequent 'Out in the Green' festival in Dinkelsbuhl is a pleasure to watch with the crowd eating out of the palms of John's hands, the trade mark cross-swords finalé of the two guitars, and Tommy smiling and thrashing away as hard as he could go to bring *Straight Forward* to a close. In Dinkelsbuhl too they finally had the thrill of meeting lifetime guru Rory Gallagher. Pat remembers the occasion

> We idolized him. We have always been ambassadors for the Irish players. We have always idolized, absolutely worshipped Rory above all. Never mind Gary Moore and Thin Lizzy. Rory was *the* man.

Meanwhile back in the UK a tape of Airrace had arrived at the Harrowby Street band HQ with a message that the singer, Keith Murrell, was now 'doing time. ' John's reaction was to ask 'What for? What prison is he in?' In fact he was performing in the musical *Time* on the West End, and so Phil Begley and Pat went to the Dominion Theatre and waited outside the stage door until he came out. When he eventually appeared they asked him 'Are you Keith Murrell? Have a listen to this. So he went away home and loved it. ' Before long Keith was in the band and was a welcome addition too being, in Michael Deeney's estimation, 'a great singer and a good guy. ' With the combination of that hit single Pat was still working on, and the perfect front-man to perform it, Wembley awaited. Michael had watched it before with Tina Turner who

Pat provided the solo for Sam Fox's Touch Me.

had played to a few thousand people a night until a handful of hits came along and changed her into a superstar. Deeney was sure that Mama's Boys were that close too, even though the clock was undoubtedly ticking.

As 1986 drew to a close the press was beginning to wonder what was happening with the start-stop career of the Irish brothers, and to observe with some concern how hard-earned momentum and prestige were beginning to trickle away. This had been the band they had championed, the one they had almost unanimously lauded as destined for the top. And though no-one had anything other than a profound sympathy and understanding for the decisions of the three brothers, the fact was, time was moving on and Mama's Boys were not. John clarified the issue and explained Tommy's illness to *Sounds* saying that he had already spent five or six months in the Royal Victoria Hospital in Belfast receiving treatment and had actually beaten this disease before. In fact he had been the only survivor of seven kids who were originally in his ward with the same problem a decade ago. Even before that, when he was nine, and when he had been given only a few months to live, hadn't he beaten the odds and gone on to live the very full and colorful life of a rock star of all things? John recounted an anecdote from his youth, emphasizing that not much had changed since those days, and reiterating the certainty that Tommy's return was imminent.

> He piped up one day and said he'd like a drum kit, and we said what the hell, we'd get it for him. It's a hard thing to have to say, but it could have been the last thing we ever got for him. He was very sick. But getting that drum kit just gave him new hope. He lives for it, he loves gigging, and without that I think he would lose the fight and the will to live.

And yet, with the best will in the world, this is not how business gets done and so the record company continued to be restless. While they were waiting they put jobs Pat's way, like recording with label-mate Page Three model Sam Fox on her single *Touch Me*. Far from being a dizzy blonde he thoroughly admired her for being 'really aware, really ambitious, she knew exactly what she was doing, what she wanted, how it was going to sound. She was listening very intently to what was going on.' His was the standard session fee of £150 (and royalties), though the hit single went to her, not his own band. John too was experiencing a whole new set of emotions on a personal level, and wanted commercial success for an entirely different reason, saying 'All I want is a hit record so I can get enough money to marry Lindy.' Lindy Benson, at the time, was a presenter for Sky TV, and lived in a flat one floor below the band at the same Beech Court address on Harrowby Street. She remembers

It was June 1987. I would see these long haired guys going in and out and it was Tommy, in his socks, who broke the ice in the hallway. He was checking for mail saying to himself 'Jaysus, nothing.' He looked like a real rocker. In a really strong Irish accent he said 'Morning. Hello, I'm Tommy. Are you in a band?' I said, 'No, but it looks like you are.' He carried on talking about his brothers, the recording, and that they'd lived upstairs for months and he made me laugh with his cheekiness.

Soon it transpired Lindy was a close friend of Olga Lange, wife of legendary Mutt Lange, who co-owned Battery Studios where the brothers were recording. That same afternoon, a chance meeting with John on the stairs led to a lengthy conversation about music. She told him about being in the Bahamas with Olga at the recording of AC/DC's *Back In Black*, and John told her about his own band's successful history. Lindy goes on

> John went upstairs to get me a rough copy of *Growing Up The Hard Way* which he wanted me to listen to, and I invited him in for tea. We talked for hours about Bob Geldof, Foreigner, Def Leppard, Clive Calder and all the prestigious managers and label bosses I had met, mainly at social dinners over the years with Mutt.

The next night they met again, went to see U2, and before too much longer were dating.

Shortly before this happened the shy, but admiring, Pat had caught sight of a member of the Tower Records management team called Sallie in a club during a break from recording *Growing Up The Hard Way*. As he had been unable to muster the courage to introduce himself however, nothing had happened, even when Tommy, who knew Sallie already, had arrived and started chatting away to her. Realizing what was going on, and appreciating that his older brother was going to need a bit of a shove, Tommy later made a phone call on Pat's behalf to her work place, but this too came to nothing. It was only some months later that the ice finally got broken when Sallie introduced herself to Pat in the backstage area of the Hammersmith Odeon during a Gary Moore gig, ironically (and mistakenly) to berate him for having urged Tommy to call her. In her reminiscences the scene then played out as follows

> Anyway, when I saw this guy for real I think something hit me too. We talked for a while, but then went our separate ways. Outside, while getting into my car, I saw two guys battling with the door of a

porta-cabin loo ... half stuck! It was Pat and Philip Begley. We got talking again and they told me they were off to see Mary Black and would I like to go too (I think they wanted the lift).

There, Philip also nudged things along a bit on Pat's behalf and so, a long chat later, a late spring day trip to Marlow for a pub lunch and -the rest is history. Both brothers now embarked on steady, long term, relationships with partners who shared a passion for music and possessed an understanding of the industry. In the fullness of time they became their wives and managers respectively.

In the studio, with Phil Begley and Johnny Fean of Horslips, the recording and production of the all important *Growing Up The Hard Way* began in earnest. But now new problems emerged with bad blood developing between the band's management and the record company. Pat remembers it clearly and the accompanying sense of foreboding that came with challenging the nepotistic ways of the industry.

Michael took us out of Battery Studios and we went down the road to Red Bus Studios where he physically made them [Jive] pay. You see Jive had put us into Battery Studios which they owned and charged us for. So they were giving us money with one hand and taking it back with the other. It was all very incestuous – from Zomba publishing (which was them) to the producers, the list is endless. We bucked the trend by going with Phil Begley who had done the earlier albums. But then he wouldn't sign up with them to effectively hand over a percentage, and so their noses were out of joint. They had to pay him, and they got nothing back. You should use the in house facilities. When we were recording at Red Bus they didn't even come down to hear how it was getting along and so we knew the writing was on the wall.

Besides all that, the music was being pushed and pulled in a variety of directions too. Begley remembers 'The record company was expecting a breakthrough in the States. We started out with the best intentions and had some good ideas in development but there was a lot of grief.' He concludes 'We somehow got hijacked by the industry and ended up compromising the work until we became exhausted and the meat was whittled away from the bones.' Though Pat had been delighted to be working with Begley again, and with the compatibility of Murrell in terms of song writing and performance, there were further problems closer to home. John remembers that when the time came to listen to the entire album played back at the studio he realized

'We were going in completely the wrong direction. ' The very music itself which had united the brothers for years was now coming unstitched under the stresses and strains of trying to write for a commercially specific and unforgiving market. If they weren't careful it might even get between them personally. And yet everyone was doing their best, everyone was fighting as hard as they possibly could with their individual demands and pressures, but it was clear, the band was losing its focus. John remembers how awkward the whole situation made him feel saying 'I respect *Growing Up The Hard Way* as a record but I remember the first time I heard it I felt like sitting down on the ground and crying. ' He looks back with regret at the cul-de-sac they had been maneuvered into saying 'We should have been more aware of what had made us successful in the early days and more in control of the decisions that were being made, instead of being steamrolled into every corner and agreeing with it. ' Pat didn't then, and doesn't today, share the pessimism about the record and reiterates 'I'm still very proud of that album. I think maybe we could have got it slightly heavier on the production side of things, but it is all very well looking back in hindsight. '

The long lay-off through Tommy's illness, the changed four-piece identity, and the musical realignment for an American market, was going to leave many of the hard-core fans out in the cold. Others asked why a talented band like Mama's Boys would release a Stevie Wonder song, *Higher Ground,* as a single at such a vital time as this? (Pat argues that it did wonders for the Red Hot Chilli Peppers when they released it a few months later, and so wasn't 'such a daft idea after all'). Those following the band closely might also have felt it odd that the brothers were no longer living in the same country, let alone the same city. As Jive had rented the Harrowby Street flat only up until the recording of *Growing Up The Hard Way* had finished, Pat and Sallie headed for Dublin (Bob Geldof's dad's old house), while Tommy flitted back and forth from London to his parents house in Derrylin and to his sister Siobhan with whom he had always had an especially close relationship. Was Pat's move to Dublin, as rumors suggested, because *Growing Up The Hard Way* was about to break so big that a move to the Republic of Ireland for its favorable tax status was advised? (Just like Def Leppard had just done). Or was it that the band of brothers was coming apart at the seams?

After a wait of almost two years Mama's Boys re-emerged into the public eye with a new look, a palpable sense of relief that Tommy was once again fighting fit, and all other problems brushed neatly under the carpet. The September 1987 issue of *Sounds* ran a story by Paul Elliott suggesting, cautiously, that the all clear could now be sounded and that this talented young band could pick up where it had left off. They had been right on the edge of global success after all and could now formally claim the heights that were rightfully theirs. In the same way that Def Leppard had waited for their drummer, Rick Allen, to make his recovery (after he lost his arm in a road accident), perhaps Mama's Boys too were now reaching the end of their involuntary hiatus. *Music Week* made the same comparison saying that both bands had stuck by their drummers when the chips were down and that such loyalty could reap only the most positive rewards. Derek Oliver was enormously sympathetic and lamented that these were 'Good guys singled out for a brutal dose of bad luck.' Mark Ashby felt that if this had not wiped them out completely, then surely they must now be invincible, concluding 'The result is a mature outfit ready for anything cruel mistress fate can chuck at 'em.' Pat was realistic about the momentum which had dissipated though, saying 'we've got no grand illusions about playing big venues. We'll hit the clubs again and build it from there.' There was no doubt, no doubt at all, that the fans and the critics were waiting right where they had been when the band had come off the road two years before and were more than ready to lap up the success that was sure to follow. Everyone it seems was rooting for Mama's Boys. And if *Growing Up The Hard Way* seemed an increasingly appropriate title for the album, then the first single, *Waiting for a Miracle*, was verging on prophetic. Pat agreed saying 'only a miracle could have saved Tommy and we still can't believe that it happened.' Now, the real test would come when they got out on the road, especially back in America -the market for which the record had specifically been written.

Mama's Boys MKII Line up: 'With the recruitment of Keith Murrell they obtained both a world class vocalist and an ongoing future.'

Chapter 5: Real Riot-House Stuff

The first major hurdle was overcome right away, and with a sigh of relief, when the critics, appreciating that there were no spare McManus brothers tucked away in Ireland, welcomed the new singer and the new line up. Enthusiastic reports started to appear about Keith Murrell noting that he had emerged from the band Airrace whose *Shaft of Light* album was already seen as something of a genre classic. Derek Oliver was keen to give Keith himself a chance to talk not only about where he had ended up but about the path that had taken him here. This, it transpired, had involved jingles, making commercials and doing recordings as a session singer. On a more serious musical note however he had worked with Lionheart, had tackled the backing vocals on Gary Moore's *Run For Cover* album, had had a fruitless time with Raid the North, and had even done a stint with Michael Schenker (in time his CV would also include The Who, Meat Loaf and Montserrat Caballé). Oliver was completely satisfied that the new arrangement made sense as

> The old three piece format seemed, in all honesty, fully played out and there appeared little chance of complete victory on a world-wide basis even though sizeable footholds had been achieved. No, the format had to be revised, and with the recruitment of Keith Murrell they obtained both a world class vocalist and an ongoing future.

Importantly, he also seemed to be able to fit into, or break into, a band of three tightly knit brothers – no easy task. Far from being an outsider Murrell recalls

> It was fantastic. Perhaps you would expect to feel a bit ostracized, or maybe find it a bit difficult to get in between them, but I never had that. I had an individual relationship with each one of them and collectively. They were such different characters that I could find something in each of them that related to my personality. I never felt like an outsider. It was based on total mutual respect.

He also made a point of explaining the very obvious musical departure from the Mama's Boys of old, and while he was at it, clarified that the entire album had already been written before he arrived. He emphasized that when Pat had first contacted him to join the band he had arrived with two cassettes of the prototype *Growing Up The Hard Way*: one with Rick Chase's vocals, the other just instrumental. All Murrell had had to do was add a vocal style to it and in this he had fitted the bill to the point that nobody had overdubbed or rerecorded a thing after the first take. Derek Oliver found all of this slightly hard to believe and coaxed Keith to concede 'To be honest, the songs are in exactly the style I would have adopted if I had been in the band from the start.' Elsewhere he reiterated the affinity and told Maggi Farran 'It almost feels as if the album was written for me. Even though I took no part in the writing it's exactly the direction I wanted to go in.' Even today he insists

> There is still a lot of confusion about me coming into the band and taking it in a more AOR direction. That whole album was already written before I was even asked to do it. I just added my interpretation. They had already decided between themselves and Jive that that was the direction they wanted to go in. It was purely the guys' decision and I was the vehicle to make that happen.

For future reference however, he told Georges Amann, everything would be penned by Pat and himself. The former clearly relished the idea saying in retrospect 'We were very compatible as writers, on the same wavelength.' *Hard Rock* Magazine in France also published an interview with Murrell which cited his key influences as Paul Rogers, Glenn Hughes, Lou Gramm and Robert Plant -exactly the gravelly, bluesy, smoky influences the brothers had been looking for. The gamble, it appeared, was paying off. The enforced lay off during Tommy's convalescence, and the search for a new singer, had given the band the luxury of time to write, think, record, re-record and over all, mature. In the New York based *Hard Rock / Metal* John also said that the songs on *Growing Up The Hard Way* had been modified on the road in a kind of trial and error system, and that this record was the polished result.

On the other hand there were those who didn't like what they were seeing, or hearing, at all, and felt that the whole thing smacked of a commercialism that only a record company could have engineered. How could this have happened to Mama's Boys they asked, and who was to blame? John doesn't mind facing up to his responsibilities

> It would be easy for me to sit here and point the finger at Jive, but we had to accept the changes as well which meant they needed to be discussed with us. In fact we were very lucky that Jive hung onto us for that two years. It was probably out of sympathy for our position with Tommy that they hung in there.

What emerged, in other words, was good but in John's opinion a different beast entirely to the one that had taken them to this point. He remembers

In 1987 we came back, but with all the wrong sounds. It sounded great, so polished, but I just didn't recognize us in it at all. For what it is, *Growing Up The Hard Way* is a good album, but it wasn't us.

And while Pat concedes that 'It wasn't Mama's Boys' he then follows the statement up immediately with 'it was definitely a road we were very happy to experiment on. ' Philip Begley also remembers being caught between a rock and a hard place, saying 'It was an extremely trying period when we were doing our best to please everyone and somehow not pleasing anyone.' When John looks back on the whole episode there is more than a hint of frustration evident in his voice when he sums up 'We already had what we needed to be a success, found a style that separated us from anybody else, but we were the last people to recognize that. ' Even the cover design for the LP fell short of the mark being presented *fait accompli* without any consultation whatsoever. Anyway, John said, 'You feel like you are being a bit of a knob when you reject everything and, in any case, they print up what they want. ' Pat, putting it down to the decisions of old management now departed, and not wanting to make too much of it anyway, quipped 'You could say we've turned over a new sleeve. '

But it was no time for jokes. Opinion was split amongst Mama's Boys fans and even within the band itself. Some thought the new direction was both timely and astute in preparing for a stellar future. Others could not help but feel that the record company had taken a product, stripped it down, re-built and re-packaged it, and were now selling it to a commercial audience unlikely to understand the subtle and nuanced music that had hitherto earned the boys so much respect. One particularly cruel journalist commented that he didn't know why Tommy had bothered to struggle with his illness if this was all that had come of it. In interviews Pat and John papered over all of the cracks and put on a united front claiming that with *Power and Passion* they had been under a lot of pressure from their record company to create a metal sound that they weren't really that proud of. This record was the antidote to all of that, a homecoming that the fans would love, and an album that really deserved the previous album's title. It was a welcome move away from the metal influences which had been shining through in *Power and Passion*, away from advice other people had been giving them, and back to a bluesy basics with which they felt so much more comfortable. Pat called the new sound 'straight down the line sophisticated rock and roll with no punches

Keith and John Live: 'These guys look set to take doors off their hinges.'

Alan Nelson on keyboards.

pulled' while reiterating that being from Ireland 'we've never been short of a good tune. ' He concluded confidently 'We're not making any excuses this time because we did everything to crack it and obviously it didn't work, so we thought to hell with it, let's give it a shot this way. ' Dave Ling's high profile article was not entirely convinced however and talked about a new 'American Feel', while other reviewers insisted that there was clearly the 'gloss & sheen' needed for the US market. Derek Oliver at *Kerrang*, loyal as ever, was not going to waste time quibbling and instead demanded 'Where the heck are Mama's Boys, that potent power-trio who released a pack of pulverizing platters and once threatened to take the entire world by storm?' His rhetorical question was answered when simultaneously he announced their re-emergence, and the musical result of it, as 'utterly staggering', being the perfect combination of Ratt and Airrace. The resultant 4 K *Kerrang* review was unstinting in its praise starting with 'Back from the gloom and despair of two years spent in the wilderness, the new Mama's Boys sound is stronger, sleazier and more spine-chilling than ever before. ' The new singer was endorsed fully too as 'the old boogie power trio formula had about as much potential as Dumpy bedding Anita Dobson' (ie possible, but pretty unlikely to go all the way). The new cocktail instead, interwoven with stylistic snippets of Survivor, Toto and Mothers Finest, 'oozes energy and vitality, yet retains that classic Mama's Boys blues breaking grittiness, ' making it 'utterly indispensable. ' Murrell was 'the jewel in the crown' when he 'takes the hookline into the stratosphere, loops the loop, and pilots it down to a smooth, soft, soulful landing. ' Thankfully most journalists and fans were equally keen to give Mama's Boys MKII the benefit of the doubt. Jon De Leon of *Hot Press* reported enthusiastically 'Mama's Boys aren't as easily recognizable as they were. If you give it a chance (and many won't) you'll realize that there is quality in them-thar vocals. No more knocking from the outside, these guys look set to take doors off their hinges. '

Everyone knew that Mama's Boys had always been a live band. Record companies could do what they wanted in the studio but the fans knew that the stage belonged to the brothers, and their new colleague, and felt sure they would not fail to deliver. To replicate Phil Begley's keyboard sounds from the studio Tommy's friend Alan Nelson, previously with Jagged Edge and Robin George, was brought in for the live shows. With a mini Irish tour to get things warmed up in October 1987 (following some intense rehearsals in Damian's shed in Dundalk), then a rampage through the UK in November, all fears were allayed. Mama's Boys, with a support act called No Hot Ashes (featuring Steve Strange on drums), were back in style. The *Carrickfergus Advisor and East Antrim Gazette*, in an article called 'Miraculous Mamas', reported that Murrell's singing 'soars through the air with the precision of a falcon with its eye on a tasty morsel', but noted too that the 'earthy folk boogie and the fiddle' had almost completely disappeared. Derek Oliver's review from the Whitla Hall in Belfast sensed nothing but the old excitement and breathlessly claimed 'Talk about being caught in a mosh, this was more like being squashed under the armpit of a giant sweaty Sumo wrestler. ' The crowd he described as 'rabid' and this made him wonder why Mama's Boys would ever play anywhere else. Importantly, he believed, a lot of this 'Real Riot House Stuff' was down to Murrell, his voice, and the new stage presence that he brought to the ranks. After 'a blast furnace encore' he concluded that Mama's Boys would surely be 'propelled to heights never previously contemplated. ' Richard Heggie felt the same way having witnessed them at the Edinburgh Venue (with Tigertailz supporting), and so concluded that 'Mama's Boys still have everything it takes to be huge. How about it?'

If Murrell had been nervous as an Englishman playing in Dublin and Belfast, it had evaporated immediately with the enthusiasm of the audiences there, and with what a French journal reported as his *sacre challenge*. In turn the new singer thanked the Dublin crowd 'for putting the album in at number 4', and the Whitla Hall audience for 'making me feel welcome. ' He recalls today

> I was nervous coming into the situation. I knew the band was so established, they were so tight, a family, and the fans were very loyal. But the relationship with the guys was so great that we could push all of that to one side and go out there. I knew there would be a little bit of flack, but you know what, I didn't mind.

After the Astoria show in London the band took *Metal Hammer* writer Harry Doherty out for a meal, explained to him all that had been going on, then let him do the talking for the eager readership of the magazine. Though not understanding why Samson had been kicked off the bill at the last minute, and absolutely hating 'the bloody fiddle', he could not help but observe that the London crowd had gone berserk ('Fast' Eddie Clarke was no fan of the violin either, charismatically recalling 'I saw them in Sacrimento and was heavily impressed. I thoroughly enjoyed it. But not the fuckin' fiddle. It was like an alien from another planet. Spare me man'). Describing the new Mama's Boys as 'crisp, calculating rock', he went on to praise Begley's production, and Murrell as 'the perfect vehicle to interpret the songs': a rising

(Above) Keith
and Pat live:
'We were very
compatible as
writers – on the
same wavelength.'

Pat on the
Growing Up The
Hard Way tour:
'The new Mama's
Boys sound is
stronger, sleazier
and more spine-
chilling than ever
before.'

star who would 'undoubtedly [be] a major vocalist for the future.' Doherty was positively effervescent when he wrote 'if this wasn't one of the best gigs I have witnessed this year then Liverpool are a fourth division side.' More than satisfied as he was with 'a catalogue of ripping ear-shredders' he could reassure his readers that even if the LP sounded a bit tame and mixed-down the live shows did not. He concluded 'They've grown up in style, but retained all the power and passion of what's gone before. Welcome back!' Lastly he threatened to publish no more Doro posters if people didn't get out and buy *Growing Up The Hard Way* which he had just made album of the month. You can't get a much more solid endorsement than that.

To this day Pat has nothing but positive memories of Keith's contribution to the band, concluding 'He was good live, and it worked well. He knew how to handle a stage.' Importantly, Murrell remembers that it was 'John who was perhaps the most encouraging' even if, in the latter's memory, there was a very awkward transition

Whether I was having vocal problems or not, it didn't matter to the fans. They didn't want to hear anybody else. In Northern Ireland they'd stick their head into the venue and say 'Hello Keith, you're a great little singer but you don't fucking belong in this band.' We had to try and get him to forget about this stuff.

Clearly experiencing his own personal discomfort and disorientation with Mama's Boys' new format, John also remembers 'I felt very out of place in the band, I didn't even know what to do with myself on the stage. I really didn't know how to work this.' But none of it was obvious to the public who were packing out gigs all over the country. To them Murrell had fitted in beautifully. Pat had also changed his solo spot into a less elaborate guitar showcase in *Last Thing at Night* and an 18h century Irish tune, *Moorlough Shore*, leaving a *Kerrang* reviewer to marvel at 'true expression and the touch of a master. I was spellbound.'

At about this time some articles mentioned a 'failed single', *Waiting for a Miracle*, which, it was claimed, 'again exposes the injustices of Radio One's airplay decisions.' The *Sunday World* in particular ran a piece called 'When a Loser is a Winner!' in which they reported that a tune called *Spirit of America* had been written for the album and earmarked as the long-awaited breakthrough single for the USA, then inexplicably canned. On closer inspection these turned out to be the same songs in slightly different formats. Manager, Michael Deeney, picks up the story

Spirit of America was 'that song. ' It had all the hooks and panache required to break the States – no doubt. I thought it was great. We thought this would give them their breakthrough. But Jive and ICM in America did not like the lyrics as they were too 'pro-American. ' Rockers are supposed to be angry rebels and this was too 'nice.' It was said it 'sounded like a Chevrolet ad. '

So while the lyrics were too pro-American for America, the tune was not European enough for a UK market, and therefore unusable on Radio One. In short, it fell between two stools. Accordingly, Pat tackled the job of rewriting the words so that it could finally be released as *Waiting for a Miracle* (complete with free cardboard fold-out guitar) and when this happened it entered the rock charts at a very reasonable Number 11 (also in the top 15 that week was *Welcome to the Jungle, Girls, Girls, Girls* and *Mony Mony*). In the meantime however Jive went ahead and released the original *Spirit of America* in the US, now performed by Sam Fox and featuring K.K. Downing and Glen Tipton from Judas Priest on guitars. Surprise was then compounded with frustration when it actually went down well and was reported positively to be 'more American than pumpkin pie. ' Even if Pat loved the idea of 'the guys from Judas Priest playing my tune', it seemed incomprehensible as a marketing decision to have the same song released twice, simultaneously, with different words. Michael Deeney understood the seriousness of the situation knowing that this time their big chance, perhaps their last chance, at a breakthrough had been bungled. Soon things went from bad to worse and Pat recalls that even though '*Waiting for a Miracle* was picking up heavy rotation in America, they wouldn't let us out. It was picking up mainstream radio play but they were having none of it. ' Murrell's recollections are similar

> In retrospect that was an absolute and complete nonsense. The single was top ten requested and the video had medium rotation on MTV. It was a foregone conclusion that the record was going to be something of a hit. And then suddenly it just dropped out and we couldn't understand it. The reason was you couldn't buy it. It wasn't in the shops.

Reading between the lines there was a growing suspicion that the record company was beginning to feel that they had invested enough, for long enough, in Mama's Boys and that it simply was not good business sense to commit another dime. All doubt was removed in Bristol on the third night of the UK tour when Michael Deeney broke the news that the record company would not be supporting the American tour. Pat insists 'We should have been allowed to get out there and work America. That is where it was geared for. It wasn't geared for England.' He also appreciated the far reaching consequences of the aborted tour and that for Mama's Boys, in all probability, 'the writing was on the wall.' John remembers the scene in a similar way

> It came as a real blow I can tell you. Michael told us in Bristol that we were not going out to America. When we heard that we knew it was bad. They had been so desperate to break this band in the States. That's when I knew it was over, finished.

The end was not long in coming. Even with the single *Higher Ground* at number 2 in the *Metal Hammer* readers' chart (behind Leppard's *Hysteria* and in front of Whitesnake, Aerosmith, Guns n' Roses and Motörhead); *Growing Up The Hard Way* in the same charts at number 5 (behind Black Sabbath, Whitesnake, Def Leppard and UDO, but in front of Kiss, Rush and Dio); with 20,000+ album sales in the first few months of release, and with two successful UK tours behind them, Jive took the fatal decision to drop Mama's Boys. John looks back on it today

> They just didn't renew the contract. It wasn't broken. We had known all the Jive people as friends, personally, stayed at their houses and played with their kids, and then, without so much as a phone call from any of these guys we were told through our manager 'your deal is gone.' That was a right wake up call.

With time to be angry, disappointed and wise in hindsight, John now knows where they went wrong and why this shattering decision was made. He makes his point lucidly

> We should have been strong enough to stand up for our own beliefs and tell them to fuck off when we didn't like what we were recording, the direction we were being pushed in, and being aware of the groundwork we had achieved on our own up to this point. We should have stayed true to our own beliefs and delivered an album that the fans wanted to hear and fuck the record company.

Pat is more pragmatic in his regret when he says

> We should have hung about in the studio running up the bill so that the record was so expensive that they would have had to push

it and make a success of it to get their money back. But instead we got it done quickly and so the record company didn't feel like they would lose too much anyway by letting us go with almost no effort to promote the work.

With cynicism he now re-assesses his relationship with the record company and concludes 'They exploit you and when they've finished they discard you.' The boys' mother, Valerie, also unhesitatingly blames the record company saying with finality 'They ruined it. They weren't allowed to do anything their own way. ' She even remembers how when her sons came home to the farm house and played a demo 'I went out to the kitchen and cried.' Concluding with the statement 'You're only a commodity to them' she mourns the time spent with people who just did not understand that this was art, and shrugged 'It is horrible to do that to artists of their caliber who were so into their music. ' Michael Deeney wraps the episode up by saying that there is no great mystery in why Jive did not renew the contract. It was 'a straight economic decision. ' Chris Tsangerides, like so many others, found it hard to believe that this was it; that this was the end of the road for the band he had been so sure was on its way to the very top. Today he remains stumped about what happened and why their success, though so often promised, was doled out to less deserving bands. When pushed for an explanation he says 'Nobody knows. If we knew that we would all be millionaires. ' Pat has the final word 'Honestly, in the music business when you are riding high you cannot afford to take two years out and we did. We never recovered from it and that was the end. '

With the record deal gone Keith Murrell jumped ship. Pat harbors no resentment saying

> He had financial commitments and he had to make ends meet. It is as simple as that. He was a working guy, he had to deliver. When we were signed that was one thing, but when we weren't, he committed the best he could but it was not enough. I've got nothing but good things to say about Keith.

Murrell himself looks back with disappointment, bewilderment, but also a sense of pride in what was actually achieved. About the boys he says

> Never was there a band more deserving of success. Not only because of their amazing talent, but because of their attitude toward the business and to people, and the fact that they just enjoyed every minute of it and had so much enthusiasm for everything. Those guys

Tommy with nurses in Belfast: 'Rock n' roll is the best medicine.'

Graham Smith

did everything right. They never upset anybody. They never trod on anyone's toes. They never had a problem coming up with the right songs ... so what else were they to do? They really were the nice guys of rock n' roll.

Michael Deeney also remembers Mama's Boys as 'incredibly hard working, dedicated lads, who always delivered, and a band made up of friendly, likeable guys', before concluding 'I couldn't fault them.' Neither could he, as a business man, keep on managing them.

An optimist, or a millionaire, might have seen this new found liberty as a chance to take stock, determine where to go next, assess the road traveled so far, and cherish the opportunity to move in precisely the direction they now wanted to go in. But that was not pragmatic thinking and Pat remembers vividly the fall from grace and the sense of absolute frustration, coupled with humiliation, when 'You had to go down to the dole office and the man there says "Didn't I see you on MTV last week?" and you say, "No, it wasn't me".' It was time, Pat concluded, for him and Sallie to head back to Dublin.

The one real ray of hope, in fact the most important thing of all to help keep things in perspective at a time like this, was the fact that Tommy's health was continually on the up. Now 22 years old and aware of the fact that once again he was beating the odds, he took the opportunity created by the break to go back to the hospital in Belfast to see the nurses who had been looking after him and told them 'I've never felt better in my whole life. I've been in remission for three years and it's for good this time -though nobody can be sure.' He extended his visit to the Hematology Unit at the Royal Belfast Hospital for Sick Children and then Ward 22 trying to lift other sufferers' spirits. *Kerrang*'s Paul Elliot reported jovially 'He's back in Ireland today, having a checkup ... and getting his leg over. Just what the doctor ordered.' Tommy even agreed to do a television interview with Shay Healey on the subject of his leukaemia which was especially unusual as, in Pat's recollections 'he could never be serious for long enough in an interview. Any interviews he did for television ended up with him being cut out. He just took the piss.' Now he talked to Healey about his illness, answering tough questions like 'Are you afraid of dying?' with a smile, a sip of a drink and a quip that 'Nah! I'll be here until I'm 70, in the pink.' This was vintage Tommy: in a bohemian hat, wearing long earrings, and beaming a huge smile while insisting that his health was 'brilliant.' He veered into some serious territory when he started to explain that this was his third time in remission and that 'normally if you fall back you usually don't get back in, but I've been really lucky. It's three years now.' He also refused to be anything other than positive about the future saying 'I'm one determined person. I love life to the last and I love touring. And I feel, only for that, I wouldn't be here. ' Healy then asked 'What keeps you going?' to which Tommy replied candidly 'Just the fact of being alive and overcoming what I did. It just gives me the adrenaline to keep going. No matter what happens, I'll fight it. ' With a cheeky smile and an equally mischievous glance he finished the interview saying 'Rock n' roll is the best medicine. '

Now a new search began for a manager, a singer, and a record deal. The former was finally found closer to home than anyone really expected. Lindy, John's partner, had a formidable list of friends who were successful managers, such as: Trudy Green (Jacksons, Aerosmith and Whitesnake), Peter Mensch (AC/DC, Def Leppard and Metallica), Colin Johnson (Status Quo), and Bud Prager (Foreigner). None of them could be convinced to take Mama's Boys on however and so six months later Trudy Green said, in a long distance phone call from Los Angeles

> Darling, why don't you manage them? How do you think I started? There are no exams. There are very few women managers, but we are good. Me, Wendy Dio, Sharon Osbourne. You'd be great.

John also thought it was the perfect solution and eventually convinced her to take the band on in conjunction with another business associate of hers in Switzerland called Graham Smith with whom she shared responsibilities. When the new management team rolled up their sleeves in 1989 and started to examine the paper work of the previous years methodically, they soon reached the conclusion that for all the McManus brothers were talented musicians they were hopeless businessmen in a cut throat industry -and seemed to care about it even less. Lindy got to work reading up on relevant music laws, attending management seminars, and absorbing every book available on the music industry, while Graham, an accountant already involved in book publishing, explored royalty splits, licensing, pressing and distribution issues. Next, £10,000 was invested in making new quality demos at Red Bus studios with Keith Murrell singing and Philip Begley producing (assisted by his engineer Pearse Dunne). It was felt that labels might be more attracted to such highly polished production as it would require so little time and investment to 'finish off. ' But this too came to nothing as record companies were literally swamped by hopefuls and rarely listened to what they had been sent, let alone new demos from a band that had recently been dropped. Paul McCartney's lawyer at Sheridans (who also handled Iron Maiden) told Lindy that however successful Mama's Boys had been in the past there was no way to start at the top again. They would just have to get out there and play and hope to be seen by someone who could make a difference. In the meantime both Pat and John had to take temporary day jobs, something Tommy was unable to do through renewed illness.

The singer situation was also hard to crack. Indeed it was even unsure whether Mama's Boys needed a new singer at all. Wouldn't this be the perfect opportunity to go back to the old formula now that no-one was twisting their arms? John has no doubt

> We should have gone back to The Shed and written the follow up as a three piece. I was the singer in Mama's Boys when we got our record deal, and I was the singer in Celtus when we got our second record deal …. [but] my confidence was gone.

Chris Tsangerides agreed and spoke highly of John's voice and the unique contribution it made saying 'That was the boys. That voice, you either like it or you don't. I loved it. ' Pat didn't see the point of going back to the old formula though believing that that decision had already been made once and didn't need to be dragged up again. And so the lengthy process of auditioning began. Lindy recalls

> I placed ads in *Kerrang* and *Music Week*, put the word out to anybody who'd listen, and soon tapes were arriving daily. It was a bit like that scene in *The Commitments* -the number of people in and out of the door. One guy could only sing if he had bright blue spandex on.

Eventually a completely unknown vocalist called Connor McKeown, from Irish rock act No Sweat, sent a tape which caught Pat's eye. Though he was undoubtedly talented, and certainly more than happy to join the brothers, both Pat and John now look back on hiring him as a mistake. Pat remembers 'he was great, he could do it, but his mindset was that he wanted to move on to bigger and better things, and fast. ' John is less charitable, saying 'that was a stupid mistake … I don't know what we were thinking.' In any case by July 1989 the *Sunday World* could make the triumphant announcement 'Mama's Boys Back on the Road Again' with Connor McKeown taking the microphone and ex-Ozzy Osbourne and Rainbow man Don Airey on keyboards. Simultaneously, a long-term Mama's Boys fan from Northern Ireland called Steve Strange, having hung up his drum sticks with No Hot Ashes, and turned his hand to being an agent, called Lindy and asked 'What about doing a show in Ballyronan with Rory Gallagher, Dumpy's Rusty Nuts, Dare, Elilir, The Mockers, Emerald and

Krakatoa?' In addition to the festival he reckoned he could get a further ten dates in England and maybe Ireland at which they could just about break even, perhaps even turn a profit depending on merchandise sales. Operating out of his 'office', which was the size of a phone box in the Elephant and Castle, Steve undoubtedly, had an eye for an idea that would sell and was not afraid of the hard work that would have to be invested to see it fulfilled. In his words Mama's Boys were 'a true road animal' and that, precisely that, was the forté of the band and its selling point. Adrian Duffy, their loyal tour manager of eighteen years, was re-recruited for the shows and Steve filled the last space available on the tour bus.

When Mama's Boys wound their way back to the UK and to the Marquee in particular, it was an instant and complete sell out. It was obvious that the fans on both sides of the Irish Sea had not deserted the band despite the interminable difficulties they had been facing. Pat joked in a television interview that they had brought them all across on the ferry and that now that the place was, in one journalists words 'like the Black Hole of Calcutta', they could relax. Graham flew in for the gig and hired a professional film cameraman to record it, but depressingly all eleven invited A&R (Artist & Repertoire) reps from labels didn't turn up, as, quite possibly, they had now come to regard Tommy's illness as a disability and the band a risky proposition. Lindy complained to the Chairman of CBS, who immediately arranged an appointment with Muff Winwood who concluded dismissively 'They should have been born in America, they are more for the US market. That's where they should move to.'

For all that McKeown proved that he was a good front man at the Marquee, it was soon blatantly obvious that he was inexperienced and so the new relationship was going nowhere. Pat smiles as he remembers 'He wanted to become the next Johnny Logan. He saw his path via the European Dress Making Competition. He wanted to sing in the Eurovision Song Contest – bad news. We didn't want to make mugs of ourselves like that.' Before long the brief relationship was over and Connor was gone. Now, perhaps for the first time, morale dipped seriously as the enforced search for yet another singer began. It was to last nine long months in which time Graham, as an investor, was becoming increasingly impatient.

Though time was very much against them as a band, every month that passed saw Tommy getting stronger and stronger. The press followed his recovery closely and reported how, unbelievably, he was beating the odds and fighting back yet again. How many times could he pull this off? Though the drugs and treatment had brought him down, and though his weight had plummeted and his hair fallen out, he had stayed eternally optimistic.

With new singer Connor McKeown at Lough Neagh.

New singer Mike Wilson: 'Velvet and leather tones.'

Most people can't survive the treatment, let alone the illness. So you've gotta be pretty strong. The worst part was I used to have the longest hair in the band, and I was well proud of it. I woke up one morning and went to brush my hair, and every bit of it was coming out. I rang up Pat, pretty much crying, and he said 'Ah, don't worry, it'll grow back.' And it did.

The *Daily Star* ran a far-fetched story under the banner 'My Battle for Life by Tommy', which reported that a 'pin-up rock drummer' who had spent four years in hospital fighting leukaemia after playing with Deep Purple, was back to full fitness, and now the 'manic drummer' (who had had vodka smuggled into hospital for him) could state triumphantly 'I wanted to stay alive to play drums – and meet girls.'

At around this time Lindy also activated a fan club and hunted down the press who soon were receiving reports of the boys buying their own London studio (and of returning to a more Gaelic form of music). In reality this was a mews house in Marylebone, paid for by Graham, which had an irresistible 29 foot basement with a cavern-style curved ceiling, and walls four feet thick. Lindy says

> It became a band house, an office, for meetings, rehearsals, interviews, accommodation, songwriting and recording. The studio was cute, red carpet, red sofas, red coffee table and everyone that entered it remarked on the cozy atmosphere.

Graham also arranged for Pat to do some session work with John Parr (of *St. Elmo's Fire* fame) in Germany. This was on a movie soundtrack for a film called *Butterbrot* produced by Harald Kloser who later went on to write, produce and compose the music for blockbusters such as *Independence Day* and *2012*, amongst others. The track *Always On My Mind* emerged, and led Parr to conclude impressively 'Music flows through Pat just as sure as the Irish blood in his veins.'

Eventually real hope was rekindled when a new singer by the name of Mike Wilson was found and recruited. This was a musician from Redcar who was allegedly managed by Led Zeppelin's iconic manager Peter Grant, had worked with Jon Bon Jovi and Richie Sambora (indeed they were playing on the demo he sent to Mama's Boys), and who was from the Coverdale / Rogers 'school' of singing. Pat loved the 'smoky, industrial blues voice' and welcomed the prospect of collaborative songwriting when it came to the new album. The snag was that for all Wilson had been a successful session singer in the past, he had never, in fact, played live. Pat recalls that Mike was a nervous wreck before the first gig and that when he discovered his secret (just before going on), he got more than a bit jittery himself thinking 'Oh no! Why didn't you tell us?' John remembers more or less the same thing

> Mike wasn't entirely truthful with us about his experience as he hadn't ever sung live in his life before. At the first concert in Austria the guy was shaking in his boots. He wasn't able to pace himself on stage either through nerves. He had this burst of energy right at the beginning and then he had nothing else left to offer, which was just inexperience.

Wilson had a few criticisms of his own and told a journalist that even though the McManus brothers were placid and confidence inspiring guys to work with, when they got onto a stage they became 'like Tasmanian devils. ' In fact, he said, having been hit by guitars, poked in the eye with violin bows, and nearly blown up by spark bombs, he took the decision that someone had to choreograph the performance to bring some order (and safety) into the live chaos.

Minor glitches aside then, there really was room for optimism one last time, and with it, the will power to give the band one final push to the top, even if the summit was substantially further away than it had been a few years before. The *Sunday World* in their article 'Mama Mia – They're on their way' agreed fully, reporting on successful Irish gigs, a headlining appearance in Switzerland, a rendez-vous with old allies Hawkwind in Mildenhall, and then a high profile sell out at the Astoria in London. Ten dates with Magnum and Blue Oyster Cult, followed by another ten alone in Austria, then wound up with a further nineteen gigs in the UK. The journalists and critics flocked to the shows, interested to see how the label-less band was faring and how their attitudes, and indeed music, might have changed. *Metal Hammer* ran a review by Pippa Lang which said that even if the three piece was now a five piece it really didn't matter as there was still a surfeit of smiling, dedication and talent. Lang saw them again at the Marquee and hatched her own theory, that because 'The McManus Brothers and Co wouldn't hurt a fly' they hadn't the marketability of Mötley Crüe or Twisted Sister. That said, their music took no prisoners and so they remained 'the only band I know who can be joyful and angry all at the same time. ' Sean Tyler spoke for many after the Marquee show saying that 'the cockles of my heart were glowing nicely on gas mark 4', commenting that Wilson was

Mama's Boys MKIII with manager Lindy Benson.

Runaway Dreams live in France: 'British Rock needs Mama's Boys and I'm glad to announce we've got 'em back, big time.'

a 'Paul Stanley/Pete Jupp clone with a Cheshire cat grin', and concluding 'British rock needs Mama's Boys, and I'm glad to announce we've got 'em back, big time. ' Andy Hughes of *Kerrang* was elated with the 'velvet and leather tones' of the new singer, combined with his 'instinctive skill and an infectious ability to enjoy the whole shebang. ' So convinced was he of their prospects that he concluded 'If there is any justice, the UK will embrace some home-grown talent for a change, or else Mama's Boys will head off to become sickeningly wealthy in sunnier parts. Don't say you weren't told in plenty of time. ' Musically it was also clear that although they were mercifully free from the priorities of the record company, very few 'oldies' were making it back into the live set. Pat declared that this was hardly a mystery as 'We thought we were writing better songs. Better, fresher, newer. It may have been stupid to think like that as the old songs meant a lot to different people, but we weren't really aware of it. '

Further afield Chris Welch from *Metal Hammer* caught up with 'the merry bunch of wandering minstrels' on the road in Buchs in alpine central Europe, where Pat talked openly about the three years that had passed since they toured there last. This hiatus, he figured, had in many ways been a blessing as it had given them the time, amongst other things, to play some live shows with Saxon (from which Biff recalls 'came a lasting friendship'). A new keyboardist, Dillon Tonkin, had been, in Pat's recollection, 'thrown in at the deep end with almost no notice, learned the set, and then recorded the live album. 'The concerts in Spain, Switzerland and England were then produced by Jean-Bertrand (Bebert) Gonnet into *Live Tonite* which was pressed on Graham's CTM label. When the *Sunday World* announced 'Mama's Boys Back to 'Earth' with New Album' in July 1992 optimism abounded. The queues at Tower Records in Picadilly for the album signing, and the very elaborate photo shoot with legendary lensman Ray Palmer, certainly suggested that the boys were back – if they had ever really been away.

Behind the scenes however Mike was causing some concern as he seemed unhappy to be on the road, the very place where Mama's Boys belonged. John remembers

> Even before concerts you would see him walking around with his head down and you would think 'What is going on in your head?' The chemistry was wrong, he was moping around, and it was impossible to get it going onstage when a member of the band felt like that. Mike was a really difficult guy to be around. He had a lot of demons, a lot of issues.

Mama's Boys have tasted the sweet elixir of success and experienced the trials of a brother and band member's fight back from leukaemia. For them to come back at all is remarkable. That they still produce top quality music is a greater credit still. Chris Welch, complete with lederhosen, met up with the band in the shadow of the Alps.

Live from the Alps with Chris Welch: 'The merry bunch of wandering minstrels.'

Lindy also looks back on this combination of talent and discontentment saying that for all he had a fabulous voice and was a 'nice guy' he was also 'very insecure.' The knife cut two ways though and it was soon abundantly clear that Wilson was finding it difficult to work with three brothers, especially when they rehearsed so much and relied instinctively on the unspoken word.

Back in the studio work on *Relativity* got under way (also for the CTM label), and it was very clear that there was going to be quite a musical cocktail served up. Some home video footage shows Tommy programming drums into computers, Pat doing slide solos on the guitar and fiddling through a wah-wah pedal, and jams with saxophones and harmonicas taking place. Less obviously though, Mike was growing increasingly frustrated as he couldn't manage to get the singing quite right even if he had done it perfectly outside the studio a thousand times before. Finally, John recalls, 'He left the studio in a huff and went back up the hotel.' John followed to get him back but a row broke out at the breakfast table and Mike shouted 'You go and fuckin' sing it then' before storming off. John then followed him up to the bedroom and

> There I got the biggest shock of all. It was so depressing in there. There were four sky lights and he had blacked out every single one of them. The room was in complete darkness. Beside his bed he was scoring off days, like he was in jail, the number of days he had left to do in the recording studios. When he agreed to go back it was on the condition that it was with me only. Pat was too tough to work for (he was known to kick Jim de Grasso's kit in Zurich when he thought he was not doing his bit). Everyone had to leave the control room except me and that was the only way we got any of the vocals done on that album. Even then we didn't get them anywhere near what we knew he was capable of.

Eventually the recording in Germany came to an end, the album went into post-production in France, and the video for *Rescue Me* was shot at Brixton Academy. Creatively, the latter was a fine investment and was shown on MTV and Raw, but in commercial reality the returns did not justify the investment. Lindy observed the worrying trend

> On the one hand everyone loved the band and it opened up a new window of life, renewed old friendships, and got the wheels back in motion. But it was costing money and time. There were no benefactors.

Portrait of an artist: 'Straight down the line sophisticated rock and roll with no punches pulled.'

It was an expensive hobby which needed foreseeable returns. It was difficult trying to ignite their attention to the importance of profits and losses.

Propped up by some further financial contributions from new-found friends Etienne and Catherine Keith in France, and professionally in need of a confidence building boost, the reviews of *Relativity* more than did the trick. *Kerrang*'s Sean Tyler fore-grounded the circumstances in which the album had been made saying 'Only Def Leppard seem to have had more shit to wade through than Mama's Boys,' just as Derek Oliver had previously written 'nasty lady luck poked a spanner in the goddamn works.' Now Chris Welch agreed and signed off with

> The boys have suffered neglect, illness, theft of equipment and a particularly cruel press review that was a hurtful blow on top of everything else. If any band deserves wider appreciation and respect it is Mama's Boys -the boys who have grown up the hard way.

In case anyone doubted the arduous route so far trodden a catalogue of horrors was presented: the kidnapping, the death of Valerie, every conceivable industry horror, corruption, incompetence, sparkling offers that could have split the brothers up forever, killer diseases ... and so on. And through it all they had come out intact, stronger musically, and more mature and determined than ever before.

The music however divided the critics again. On the one hand there was a majestic diversity that encompassed 'shenanigans on the fiddle', 'boogie till you poop ditties' and 'whisky and blooze.' On the other, there was Andy Bradshaw's opinion in *Metal Hammer,* that it was dated musically and unlikely to lure new listeners being 'caught between rock and a much softer place,' and lacking real adrenalin. The flashes of brilliance remained, he conceded and, on the whole, it was good to have Mama's Boys back, but the tunes were, in his opinion, a little *passé*. Pat appreciated that and noted 'the climate musically had changed and there was really no place for the likes of our band. We were totally out, irrelevant.' He shrugs when he thinks about illusive commercial success saying 'We'd been through all of that and we decided just to be true to ourselves as it doesn't really matter anyway.' When they took the record out onto the road the crowds still loved it. Packed venues all over Europe resounded to a mixture of the old and the new alike. At the Locomotive in Paris, following a packed record signing session, *Runaway Dreams* went down a storm, while in Lyon and Lisbon the whole thing descended into a sing along chorus more usually associated with the terraces when the Irish football team is playing in the World Cup. In Vienna Mike scaled the scaffolding to squeeze the very last drop out of the festival audience, and in Montpellier *Judgement Day* went down a treat. No one but an insider could have known that tension within the group was now becoming unbearable. Niggling moments could perhaps have been spotted by the trained eye when Mike and John were being interviewed on the TV together and under duress Mike said 'You have to respect the old songs', to which John immediately shot a glance and quipped 'You don't though.' When the interviewer went on to ask what it was like not being a brother and not being Irish, Mike replied 'A nightmare.' Behind the veneer of laughter there was a bitter truth. John later recollected

He seemed to resent the past, the old songs. We would say to him 'You are in the group now so enjoy it', but Mike found it very difficult to get past that because everywhere we went he was always reminded of that. He would not sign old albums for example. Mike had great potential but whatever was going on upstairs, I do not know. He hated the past, he resented it, and yet he was part of it. We were giving him this opportunity and he was fighting it.

Then one day Mike just got up and walked out. One minute he was sitting on the sofa in the house reading the paper, the next he was gone. Pat thinks that he had fallen in love with a flight assistant and faced with a choice between her and his unhappiness in the group, had known which way to go. He continues sympathetically

Mike had personal things going on. That's just Mike. He felt slightly intimidated by the fact that it was three brothers. We didn't think it was difficult but of course it was going to be difficult. Looking back on it now we realize it was impossible. I can understand where he was coming from. He was a great singer though he never really lived up to expectations with us or with anyone else. He was a singer to be reckoned with.

Now, even though Mama's Boys had been left in the lurch yet again, John remembers feeling nothing but relief, and even experiencing an inkling of hope

It was like someone had told me I had just won the lottery. I couldn't contain my joy. I should have been devastated that Mike was gone because we were fucked. We were just about to go out on the road in three days time. I quickly went down to the studio, put the bass on, and tried to sing. There was not a chance that I was going to suggest to Pat that I would do vocals, not a chance, not ever, ever, ever. It would have to come from Pat. Secretly I was desperate to become the singer again. I really wanted to be back in my spot again and be the leader again, live.

When Pat arrived at the house Lindy told him about Mike's departure and, supported by Tommy, got down on his hunkers beside where John was sitting and said 'Do you think you could do it? Why don't you give it a go?' Within three days John was ready and 'I was loving every single moment of it again. I was excited again.' Pat enjoyed it too but wasn't so sure about the long-term viability of a return to the three piece formula.

Fate had not finished with the brothers yet though. Instead of being given some time and space to revel in the return to the old Mama's Boys, and in the excitement for the upcoming gigs in Switzerland, worrying signs suddenly began to appear again concerning Tommy's health. John realizes now that without telling anyone else

He knew how sick he was. He was not himself, a bit more down or in a trance. He was telling himself there was a problem as he knew all the symptoms. In the end he knew more about it than the doctors.

When Tommy could conceal it no longer, and when he finally admitted to himself that the problem was beginning to look very serious, he confessed his doubts to both Lindy and his brothers who immediately agreed that the band should take another break to let him get better. No decision was ever taken to finish Mama's Boys completely. Quite the contrary. There was the complete belief that as soon as he recovered they would be off again. It was just a matter of priorities and of time. In any case they knew that they had missed their shot at the big time and were more than happy to settle for a lifetime of writing, playing and touring, which was reward enough for the three brothers who had never really asked for very much more.

The very last show that Mama's Boys played therefore was, appropriately enough, back in Switzerland, fulfilling an obligation that had been contracted by Graham some time before. Full circle! This, John remembers, 'was a farewell tour without any of us knowing. Maybe it is better that we didn't know it was our last show. 'The Rain Halle, Mohlin, was packed and the gig was broadcast on National Radio, ensuring that Mama's Boys bowed

Pat live on the Relativity *tour: 'Music flows through Pat just as sure as the Irish blood in his veins.'*

(Above) Pat live on the Relativity tour: 'True expression and the touch of a master.'

Alan Williams (keyboards)

out on a high note. Crowds of music lovers had queued down the street for ages before hand and were amply rewarded when the old 'classics' like *Belfast City Blues* and *Hard n' Load* were allowed back into the set. There is some home video footage of the brothers and keyboardist Allan Williams fooling around backstage waiting to go on. In retrospect it is poignant and tinged with sadness as, when talking about the band's imminent hiatus, Tommy says 'It's a crime.' Of course seconds later the situation was diffused with another mimicked voice and a peal of laughter from everyone in the dressing room – but his comment was serious. Under the spotlight a few minutes later, and after the thumping opener of *Gentlemen Rogues*, Tommy shouted forward to John 'Welcome back mate' and in John's words 'I grew inches.' Even Bebert, the sound engineer, came up to John after the gig and said 'Look at this. The hairs on my arms are standing up for the first time since 1985.' When it was over there was no joy in taking the final bow though. Instead John remembers breaking his lifetime rule of abstinence and downing two shots of Jack Daniels as he walked off the stage.

Today he cherishes the memory of how and where the Mama's Boys story ended saying 'Once the three of us performed together again as a three piece I felt something. I hope Pat and Tommy felt the same. We never spoke about it.' At the time though he had total confidence that his brother would soon be well again and that when that happened they would continue as before. He concludes 'There was no way we were going to break up. This is what we do. Me, Pat and Tommy, together, forever.' In Milan, a couple of days after the Swiss show, it became abundantly clear that Tommy's condition was deteriorating rapidly. John now sees that 'Tommy was really dying, in all honesty.'

Tommy: 'More energy than a barrel load of monkeys and is just about as mischievous!'

Tommy and Pat with Lars Ulrich of Metallica: 'He lives for it, he loves gigging, and without that I think he would lose the fight and the will to live.'

Chapter 6: A Rare and Enduring Source of Solace and Pride

On the drive home from Italy Pat noticed that Tommy was sleeping a lot, and so when they arrived back in London Lindy immediately started ringing around and making appointments with specialists who might be able to diagnose exactly what it was that was happening now, and predict how severe it might yet become. Tommy then requested blood tests to be done in Harley Street, and waited anxiously for the results to come back. When they did, they were not good at all. Lindy remembers

> He was upstairs pacing up and down like a lion and when the lab called me and told me Tom should get back to Ireland to see his own doctor as soon as possible, I froze with fear. They didn't have to add any further details. I couldn't speak, or even say goodbye. I just hung up, numb.

Tommy: 'He just didn't care, maybe because of all that he had been through. Remember he was very young, he wasn't afraid of anyone. He'd just bound in there and shake hands. There were no airs and graces about him at all.'

Before long he was re-admitted to the Royal Victoria Hospital in Belfast where the chemotherapy began again in earnest. Though familiar with the entire exhausting process, and still utterly determined to get well again to tour and make music, Tommy began to notice odd things that he had not seen before, the most noticeable of which was a dark stripe which appeared along his arm. Perhaps, he thought, the chemo had been done too quickly and it had burned the inside of his veins, or perhaps his body was showing that it simply could not go through all of this again. To add to his concerns he was also told that another heavy dose of chemo could actually induce a heart attack. Tommy knew that this time he was in serious trouble and so allowed Lindy to get him transferred back to London, specifically to University College Hospital, which was seen to be a superior institution and so much closer to where they were living. In the interim, Lindy recalls

> I had heard through Olga that Mutt Lange had sent someone to the Bristol Cancer Care Centre as the way they prepare patients mentally for various procedures was admirable. Mutt couldn't praise them enough. Tommy and I went on a lucky last-minute cancellation and as his 'supporter' we even shared a room. I still treasure my private week with him. We talked deeply about everyone and everything but also had a total focus on all the good sensible things.

Upon their return Tommy was admitted to University College Hospital and monitoring began. As this was close by Lindy could attend medical meetings, not only as his future sister in law but as his manager, cassette player in hand, to get a permanent record of what was being said and a clear set of instructions about what to do next. Nothing however could dilute the ever-present horror of watching Tommy face the very real possibility of death, and still steadfastly refuse to admit it — at least to them. This fear was exacerbated further when the specialist forewarned everyone that further chemo was now, in fact, no longer an option and that a bone marrow match should be considered very seriously indeed. John remembers that just as Tommy's positive attitude had always given such certainty before, now was no different. Even today the incomprehensibility is still evident in John's voice when, talking of this nightmare, he says 'Jesus Christ, we knew he was going to get better. There was not a chance that Tommy was going to die. ' Tommy believed that too, utterly, and only got really frustrated or pessimistic when the doctors told him that far from touring with his brothers, he would not even be allowed to go to the studio to write and rehearse with them. Often he couldn't see the problem as there were many days when he got to live a pretty normal life. Psychologically he had become adept, long ago, at dodging the shadow of a relapse that permanently hung over him and so as the treatment started to kick in, he like those around him, allowed himself to be quietly confident that he was once again going to beat the odds. If he could kick it again this time he would buy himself a few more years at the very least. That's the way he had to think: to stay positive, to keep up appearances and to make the very most of what time he had left. John looks back and says

> When Tommy was at University College Hospital he would have pushed the drip up the road to come and work with Pat and me in the studio. He was that adamant to get out and to get back into the swing of things. It took his mind off his problems. He'd tell you anything.

Mama's Boys took no more bookings during this period as they would not countenance going out without Tommy. They did however harbour a real sense of optimism for their future as *Judgement Day* had just been selected for the opening of the World Super Middleweight Championship boxing bout between Nigel Benn and Chris Eubank at Old Trafford. A press release even quipped that the brothers were about 'to take on the heavyweights of the music industry.' Of course it seemed logical to remove Mike Wilson's vocals from the original version and replace them with John's, so he flew back to Saarbrucken in Germany, where the masters were, and re-recorded the song. He needn't have bothered as the version that ended up being aired was somehow the original with Wilson singing. Other commissions came and went, and soon the boys were writing music for the Sky Sports channel. Far more interesting was when Pat was asked to replace a classically trained violinist who had got a little out of her depth working with Tricky on the *Pre-Millenium Tension* album. A mutual friend by the name of 'English Pete' told Tricky that there was no greater man to improvise on the fiddle than Pat McManus who, when asked, responded with 'Right, ya boy ya, where's me wah wah peddle?', and flew to Malaga for the session. In the studio his only instructions were 'Just feel the vibe, and go with the flow' and so 'I just played whatever came to me as the track was going along, felt the vibe, put the wah wah on the fiddle, and it was what he was looking for.' He also played the piano on a few tracks. Quite unexpectedly Pat found an enormous respect for Tricky's approach to composition writing whereby he 'threw out the rule book on anything that you consider a format or structure.' Tricky, on the other hand, was not slow in criticising Pat's more conventional technique, and for being 'a conformist,

The Government: 'It was not the end of Mama's Boys and the start of The Government.'

which really made me think for the first time ever. ' A little wiser Pat left for home with a new found respect and more than a few new ideas from his new mentor: 'He was the most clued in person I had ever worked with in my life. I was absolutely amazed that he had such a knowledge of music. ' With his head full of new ideas about how to approach musical composition, and lyric writing, ideas that would later come to fruition with Celtus, Pat now looks back saying 'He is a poet really. The lyrics that came out were fantastic and they came straight off the top of his head. I learned a lot from him about attitude and about not being afraid to try things. '

On a larger scale, and with John and Pat working together during the wait for Tommy's return, another project was born, based on experimentation with the new Seattle sound. Under the moniker The Government a five track demo tape, hinting at Nirvana, Robert Plant, Rush, Genesis, and all the influences and styles that might appeal to readers of *Q*, was soon in circulation. But neither of the brothers cared for it at all. What was the point in heading off in a new direction when Tommy was certain to be well again soon and when Mama's Boys would be back out on the road where they belonged? In the meantime though they stuck with it, being advised to go in all sorts of directions. Pat is blunt

I always hated it. It wasn't us. It wasn't where we were coming from. It was so many people telling us 'You should be like Pearl Jam. ' I have about as much affiliation with Pearl Jam as I have with Buzz Aldrin. We were mimicking it, but it was a cheap and contrived copy of it. It meant nothing to us. It wasn't being true to ourselves. That *is* clutching at straws.

John remembers the disorientation too and reiterates the fact that The Government was never meant to be anything other than a stop gap.

The Government was just something to occupy ourselves. We didn't want to do Mama's Boys without Tommy. By this time of course the whole music industry had changed. Nirvana and Pearl Jam had come along. We felt very isolated, almost as if we had no place in the music business at this time because we couldn't really offer anything. It was not the end of Mama's Boys and the start of The Government.

A few gigs happened at the Mean Fiddler, and there was a TV appearance or two, notably on the James Whale Show, but it was never going to amount to very much more. When pushed, Pat dismisses the whole abortive project impatiently with 'We were never going to be the next Stone Temple Pilots.

Would you ever go and take a running jump,' before closing down the line of enquiry once and for all with 'I wouldn't remember anything about that because I wasn't interested in it. When I'm not interested a glaze just crosses my eyes. I've no recollection of that at all. '

In any case, the music seemed to be little more than a pass-time, a distraction, to keep Pat and John agile and imaginative for when Tommy got back out of hospital. And *there* was the problem. It was becoming very clear to doctors and family members alike that this time Tommy was not going to be able to muscle his way through using sheer will power alone. Quite the contrary. Such was the seriousness of his deteriorating condition, and such was the rapidly accelerating rate of the decline, that the doctors offered him the most dangerous of all options -the bone marrow transplant. As he was still comparatively young it was understood that he would have a better chance of resisting the trauma of the procedure, and of pulling through completely. If he left it for a few more years and was further weakened by interim medical procedures the doctors could offer no guarantees for his safety at all. Tommy knew they were right, for although one day he would be down stairs in the studio playing and writing, the next he would be throwing up blood on the side of the street. He had noticed other things starting to go wrong too and was now permanently in fear of what tomorrow might bring. Pat recalls

> He made up his mind to do the transplant. I remember saying to him at the time 'Tommy, this is a very, very, very serious step you are taking' and he said 'I know, but my body isn't going to take much more of this chemotherapy. My kidneys are not right, my liver is not right and I can't face waking up every morning and reaching under my arm to see is there a lump. I'll take the chance. '

When Tommy made up his mind, it was then time for the doctors to come clean about the very real risks associated with such a serious medical procedure and to make the family aware of the fact that two out of three recipients of this treatment do not survive. Tommy chose not to think about it in those terms and, knowing that he was out of options anyway, preferred to see it as a wonderful opportunity to kick the leukaemia, and all its dreadful symptoms, once and for all. Anyway, depending on how you interpreted the statistics, he actually had a one in three chance of making it through, and took comfort from knowing that he had beaten much worse odds than those in the past. Hadn't the doctors themselves talked about the 'miracle of his survival' before, and hadn't the newspapers even run columns on how he had fought off this spectre and come back who-knows-how-many times since he was nine years old? For Tommy the path was clear. He would undergo the operation and do so with a positive attitude and the absolute belief that he would soon be back on the road with his brothers.

The internationally respected Professor Goldstone now outlined the careful balancing act of tests, radiation and monitoring that lay ahead, and warned Tommy that as his immune system would soon be depleted by radiation, a chest infection would become a major critical risk. If all went well, and if the transplant grafted successfully, he could be out of hospital in 4-6 weeks. If he got through the first year he would be out of the woods completely and could even learn of the name of his donor. But first a donor had to be found and accordingly everyone in the family was tested. Cruel irony was compounded here by the fact that only Tommy's sister, Valerie, who had been killed in the car crash, matched his marrow type. In fact it would take a further year to find a suitable donor during which time Tommy's physical condition had difficulty in matching his fighting spirit. For example, on one occasion he told John to come and pick him up from the hospital so that they could go home and tinker in the studio. By the time John arrived he had already disconnected himself from everything and so they left together full of ideas for a project. As he turned from the Tottenham Court Road onto the Marylebone Road, however, he suddenly got violently ill, throwing up, but gasping 'I'll be alright!' Undeterred, he made it to the studio in the house and got to work using a drum pad, which required very little motion or energy, on a new composition, *Love Turns to Dust*. During another hospital stay his mother couldn't help but fret that her boy had stopped eating and was, as a result, getting weaker by the day. Weak, dosed up with medication, and using no energy whatever, it was normal that he should lose his appetite, but now he was wasting away in front of her eyes. When a young nurse told her that marijuana could not only dull Tommy's pain but actually make him want to eat, Valerie headed off in a black taxi to get some. Unsure of what it was, or where to get it, she simply told the driver what she needed and when he balked at the request she argued 'If your wee boy was as sick as mine you would do this too.' He saw the legitimacy of the mother's plight and took her to a tenement building, waited outside nervously, then drove her back to the hospital where she helped her son puff the smoke out the window. Before long his appetite was back and Tommy was eating, even if the doctors would have frowned on the 'medication' taken. Other times he was absolutely fine and the old Tommy re-emerged. Pat remembers that during these positive up swings he even used to go clubbing with keyboardist Alan Williams and Steve Strange.

In the year that he was waiting for the donor he took some treatment and some alternative treatment. He could work down in the studio quite a lot and even managed to go out to clubs from time to time. In fact he was strong before he went in for the transplant … you have to be.

After what seemed like an age, the news came that a suitable donor had been found, and so the radiation treatment to kill his own bone marrow got under way. John remembers his horror when, at the Middlesex Hospital, Tommy was strapped to a big wheel for the start of a medical procedure which eclipsed even the barbarism of the liver biopsy which had gone before. Perhaps now it began to sink in with John that, even if Tommy survived all of this, he might be different somehow. Lost in thought, and beginning to get a sinking feeling that his younger brother was never going to come out of this in one piece, he was astonished when the doors banged open 'and he came out and said "Right! Let's go! I'm feeling great". ' The process was repeated two or three times until finally Tommy's marrow was gone, at which point he was hospitalised within an Isolation Unit full time to reduce the very high risk of infection. With no immune system at all, Tommy could not fight back against even a minor infection which, in turn, might yet become deadly. Family and friends visited in relays, phone calls came in from all over the world, and Tommy's spirits remained high as the medical team made their daily reports in anticipation of what was to come.

The transplant turned out to be a mercifully humane and simple process, not dissimilar to a blood transfusion. As a slow drip of pink fluid ran through a Hickman Line into Tommy's chest he remained conscious and chatted to those around him, even if he was feeling a bit weak. His mum was there and so was his sister Molly, who was by now a nurse back in Ireland. When it was done there was nothing anyone could do but sit back and wait -counting time, not in years, but in days, possibly hours. All the early indicators were good too as the marrow showed signs of grafting. Good wishes continued to flow in from all over the world, all of which gave him and his family the strength to battle on. John remembers some less welcome wishes which served only to raise hopes before dashing them once and for all

Lots of people said he would be fine, people from the church told us that it is all just part of a test from God, testing your belief. And ultimately it was all just 'false hope. ' I wish people wouldn't do that.

As each hour passed, and each day slowly came to a close, there were sure signs that Tommy was beating the illness again. But then, despite the fact that he had been sitting up and chatting with everyone in the best of spirits for over three weeks, his eyes suddenly became bloodshot, his gums started to bleed, and he began to complain of a back ache. John recalls that Tommy 'knew immediately what that meant' and despite all his efforts could not hide the pain he was now in. John began to realise too that this was the beginning of the end for his brother and could not stop himself from crying, which only encouraged Tommy to make a super-human effort to hug him, saying 'Don't worry it will be fine.' John alerted the doctors and 'I knew by their body language they were very concerned.' What happened next was the stuff of nightmares. John recounts

It is all like a bad film in my mind now. The journey we made that night is one I will remember for the rest of my life. They needed to take him over to a different part of the hospital which was on the other side of the road. We went down in this lift -the doors opened and we were underground in the hospital in these narrow corridors … this journey seemed to go on for ever. All you could see were these lights passing by. They had sedated him at this stage to ease the pain he was in.

Having rushed through the labyrinth towards Intensive Care they eventually arrived at a room into which Pat and John were not allowed to follow. Peering frantically through the window they saw Tommy's valiant, though losing, battle continue

He could barely open his eyes at this stage, but he did, and he talked … then he attempted to try and lighten the mood. He saw Pat and me standing outside his room door looking through the glass. He slightly opened his eyes, and he knew we were upset. He made this attempt at pulling off his mask to make a funny face. Even at this point, so close to death, he was trying to make everybody else feel better about his condition. That was Tommy.

It was clear now that Tommy was dying. As a last chance, a shot at anything, John raced home and got a copy of *Love Turns to Dust* to play to Tommy and even though the doctors had induced a state of paralysis in him 'he just about managed to move his fingers.' He could hear. But it was only for a moment and soon he lapsed into a coma. Suspended between life and death, Tommy could contribute no more to this fight. After a number of further tests it became clear that he was clinically unable to support himself any longer and so the agonising decision was made, on Wednesday November 16, 1994, to switch off his life support machine. In the presence of Big John, Valerie, Pat, Sallie and Molly, John remembers the harrowing moment

> I thought he would just keep on breathing. When they switched it off I was holding his hand and you could feel his body start to go cold. When he went it was the end of my world.

Tommy's remains came home from England on a dull wet Friday and were taken to St. Ninnidh's Church in Derrylin, where Canon Liam Gaffney received them. Tommy had been baptised in this church and now his funeral was being held here too -his journey through life over. The interment took place the next day not far from where he had cycled after Barry Devlin on his BMX all those years before, and he was laid to rest beside his sister, Valerie. St. Aiden's High School Choir performed, as did a young traditional group which played 'a very moving slow air. ' John could just about manage a glimmer of gallows humour when he walked into the church and the place was like 'a sold out gig. ' He looked at Pat and said 'Well, he's still pulling them in. ' Though Tommy had lived a very full life, Canon Gaffney said in his homily 'But in the case of young people who are taken away in their youth and all the journeys they could have made remain unrealised, it is particularly sad. ' Friends, musicians and family all marvelled that Tommy had borne 'his illness with dignity and fortitude, and never lost his belief in God or his family, nor them in him. ' The priest remembered that 'he was always the same friendly and pleasant Tommy McManus with no airs and graces about him. ' It was stating the obvious that 'His departure from this life has left a gap not only in the band, but in the family circle that can never be filled. ' As he was carried out to his final resting place a guard of honour was formed by the organisations of which his family were members, such as The Mummers Group, the Historical Society, Comhaltas Branch and the Aughakillymaude Community Association. The local papers rallied round to support the McManus family saying 'They can certainly be assured of the prayers of the entire community to help them bear this, the second heavy cross they have been asked to carry. ' Tommy was, after all, a Fermanagh musician who 'has surely left behind a rare and enduring source of solace and pride. Precious and vibrant memories indeed. ' Though it was time now time to let 'his gentle, noble soul rest in peace' John was appalled at what lay ahead

The whole idea of thinking what life would be like without him … that is what was frightening the hell out of me. He wasn't just a brother, but the life and soul of the party and a really good friend. He was the driving force behind the group. It was his character that we were going to miss more than anything else.

In Prague Graham lit a candle for Tommy and at home in London Lindy eulogised him saying

He had a magnetic personality and an ability to capture any person, any age, with his incredible sense of humour. He was a gifted drummer, brilliant mimic, and had a flirty, likable charisma. His enthusiasm and passion was the glue that held the band together.

In France Etienne Keith remembers the phone call which broke the news of his death

The morning after Tommy died, I think it was a Wednesday, Lindy rang me at my office to tell me that Tommy had left and that Valerie, his mother, wished to talk to me. I didn't because what can you say to a mother that has just lost her son? But it was too late! Valerie did the whole conversation. I couldn't utter one word. She said to me in an unusual soft and gentle voice that from now on Catherine and myself are their son and daughter. And you know how deep the meaning is for an Irish family.

The French music press followed with their tributes. Laurence Faure wrote an obituary for *Hard Rock* Magazine and Jean Pierre Sabouret wrote one for *Hard n' Heavy*. London's *Kerrang* published a photo of him arm in arm with Lars Ulrich of Metallica, and Mike Edgar dedicated an hour long tribute to his life and work on the radio. Musicians rallied round too: Don Airey remembered the man, the musician and the mischief, saying 'He was one of the nicest and funniest people I have ever known in the business, and perhaps sensing he might not be around for long, lived life to the full.' Keith Murrell's memories speak for many when he remembers

a bubbly young guy, a show off, who just wanted to have a laugh all the time. On a tour bus, crammed in with crew, after hard gigs in Europe, in the middle of the night in winter, when everyone had the flu, Tommy would be standing in the door with his jacket on saying 'Are we off to the bar then? Ah come on!'

Biff Byford of Saxon lamented that Tommy 'was taken too early in life but as the song says, we will remember', while Chris Tsangerides concluded pensively that Tommy had 'such a vibrancy for life you couldn't help but fall in love with the guy. If everyone was like Tommy McManus the world would be a better place.' But Tommy was gone.

TOMMY'S VERSE

A heart of gold stopped beating when you heard God's gentle call
And taking Jesus by the hand, you quietly left us all
God saw you getting tired when a cure was not to be
He closed His arms around you and whispered "Come to me"

Each time we look at your picture, you seem to smile and say
Don't be sad but courage take, and love each other for my sake
We think of you in silence and often speak your name
All we have are memories and your picture in a frame

To us you were someone special, someone set apart
Your memory will live forever, engraved within our hearts
Our lives are all so different now from what they used to be
All because you are not here to share our company

We cannot bring the old days back when we were all together
You went to join your sister Val, to live with God forever

Tommy: 'I thought he would just keep on breathing. When he went it was the end of my world.'

Signing Celtus at EMI: 'One day I'm going to sign the boys up there.'

196   *John back on vocals with Celtus: 'A voice made in heaven that fits where they come from like a glove'.*

Chapter 7: Out of the Celtic Twilight

Tommy's death not only brought Mama's Boys to an end, it paralyzed Pat and John into complete inactivity, even for their common and all-consuming love, music. They knew, having learnt to live with Valerie's death, that there was going to be no easy way through this and that only by facing the truth head on, and together, could family and friends contemplate a future without Tommy. Healing would have to set its own pace, take its own route, and as grieving faded allow recovery to begin. Denial, regret, pity and sorrow would all have to play themselves out before anything constructive could emerge in their places. In an interview with the *Irish News* John summed up the family's torture, saying

> It was devastating for everyone. Thankfully we are a very close family and we helped one another to cope with the situation, although the hardest thing for us was to watch our parents having to go through the pain of it all.

Lindy did what she could to take care of myriad practicalities and, within the month, invited the McManus family to London for Christmas and the New Year. To coincide with this she also invited all the doctors and nurses round for an 'open house' to let Tommy's mum and dad hear all the nice things being said about their son. They had, after all, worked with each other towards a common, if unfulfilled, goal for a stressful year. But despite all of this there was no way to gloss over the agony brought about by Tommy's absence. Lindy remembers

> New Year was extremely sad. We were all still raw. Just mum and dad, Pat and Sallie, John and me. It was very hard clinking glasses at midnight. The future was completely blank.

Pat and Sallie's situation was even more emotionally complex as they were preparing for the arrival of their daughter Shannon who was now only a matter of weeks away. Perhaps inevitably Pat and John started to live increasingly divergent lives in London, reluctant to meet up, let alone revisit the places where so many memories resided. In time though, John remembers, the first glimmers of a breakthrough emerged.

One day I went for a walk and I ended up going back to University College Hospital where he had received his treatment. I took the exact same route again through the corridors across to the other side and right up outside the room where he died. I stood there for ages, just staring in and thinking about everything I had witnessed over the last few weeks. When I came out of the hospital I came out onto the corner of Grafton Way and Tottenham Court Road where you can see the windows from UCH where he would always stand, beside a Coke machine, when I was leaving the hospital and keep waving until I was out of sight. I went to Regents Park and then down to the studio where I lifted the whistle he had bought me in Dublin -it was a Low Flute -and composed this piece of music called *Brother's Lament*.

In a basement studio, alone with music, John could finally begin to harness his feelings and find a way to purge them out gradually and constructively. Music would always be the conduit through which emotions flowed when all other forms of communication and expression were blocked. Pain was no exception. Feeling some benefit from the catharsis John called Pat, but his brother wasn't yet ready to face the studio and the past. It was simply too painful, and too soon, to start moving forward again. The steps would have to be small and methodical, and so their first meeting was in the neutrality of a pizza place on Baker Street. There John told Pat 'I have written this piece of music and I would really like it if I could play it for you.' Pat eventually agreed to return to the house, to go downstairs to the studio, and to listen to his brother's composition. He remembers the moment and the tune which 'was absolutely fantastic, you could tell it was utterly heartfelt.' Instinctively he picked up a guitar and started to play along, making suggestions and adding interpretations. Slowly, the two brothers began to play and write together again, allowing the music to become imbued with a genuine love and a profound melancholy from which it could only benefit. Through music, Pat later told a TV program, they had all been given 'a chance to grieve in our own way.' Perhaps that is all it was meant to do. Pat certainly valued it as such

> These were hard days and it was a form of therapy as I had buried my head in the sand and not really talked about Tommy, because it was hard to deal with.

Not unimportantly John couldn't help but observe that through music the onset of the unthinkable had begun: 'I noticed we started laughing again and remembering the good times.'

The pragmatics of day-to-day living however, especially as a first-time father in Pat's case, meant that music would almost certainly have to remain a pastime and a private source of solace. Both brothers were trying to make ends meet with casual work which may not have been glamorous, but got them out of the house, and kept their minds off everything that had been lost. Not only had Tommy been taken away, but so had a career on stage, touring the world and making music. On one occasion, as postal sorters in Vauxhall, it all came to a head when, as Pat recalls

The two of us were sitting there taking a break at 4. 00 in the morning and who walks in but two boys wearing Mama's Boys T-shirts. We slithered down and kept out of sight. That rubbed our noses right in it.

After that Pat started working for a cleaning company. At nights he would come in exhausted, see his wife and young child, then go to the bedroom and start writing a few musical ideas here and there. With heavy responsibilities, new priorities, to say nothing of sentimental barriers, a return to the music industry remained entirely out of the question. He remembers

I had a wife, and a kid and a mortgage. Unless some kind of financial help came along there was just no way I could juggle so much: work a 10 hour day and then go in and work another 4 or 5 hours, and then go home and go to bed and get up again! It just wasn't going to happen.

And yet it did happen. Perhaps through fate playing its next, unpredictable, hand, Jonathan Czerwik, a talented and formally trained musician who had been a Mama's Boys fan for ages and who had phoned Lindy several times before Tommy's death, now re-contacted her to see if she knew of any opportunities for a keyboardist in London. Simultaneously friends, Etienne and Catherine, had also come back into the picture having secured much of the finances (£20,000 courtesy of the Smurfit family Foundation in Dublin) needed for Pat and John to quit casual work and concentrate on making a demo of these new songs. They appreciated that talent like this shouldn't be squandered and understood that at times like these a helping hand can make all the difference. Additionally they told Pat and John of a promise they had made to Tommy in their final phone call with him.

We talked a lot and he made us make the promise that, with or without him, the band had to exist and to carry on. We were in tears, as you can guess.

The poignant message was late in coming but crucial when it arrived. Etienne and Catherine went on to report that Tommy had even been coming round to a more traditional, perhaps Celtic, form of music which, if he had been spared, would have been his road of choice. In a way Pat had known this simply by watching Tommy in his final year or so.

> He was starting to come full circle. He had started to play a bit of fiddle (and was doing well), he could pick up most instruments and have a good go at it. He taught himself piano, but there was no real thought or method behind it, he could just do it.

Ironically, Pat also began to realize in retrospect that the only sort of music Tommy hadn't really listened to was the sort that Mama's Boys wrote and performed. And so taking the message and the offer of financial assistance, Pat and John quit their jobs and allowed themselves to be lured back towards music – where they belonged. Sallie looks back on these unlikely benefactors of the arts in France and states proudly

> Now we consider them to be amongst our greatest friends. Their belief in the band and the family was endless. They went the extra mile to help the guys. You remember that forever, you are indebted forever.

Free from other time consuming commitments now, the brothers gravitated towards their newly found re-acquaintance with traditional Irish music and allowed themselves to be taken a little closer to home and a world with which they were more familiar. Pat recalls that whereas this was an organic growth, and an emotional homecoming in many ways, there was also a practical element too. No longer teenagers on the road and out to conquer the world, this music was going to be mature and sophisticated.

> The heavy rock was over and done with. I thought in my own head that I was making music now that anyone could listen to. I though this is nice and refined. Rock music is always considered a bit mindless, which is not true, and this I thought was a way of getting people to sit up and listen. Now it is more sophisticated and people will not say 'Turn that noise down.'

Jonathan Czerwik was then formally offered a place in the founding line-up of the as-yet un-named band. He was only 20, knew all about programming which was a whole new experience to the brothers, and could be offered bed/board/expenses until things got up and running fiscally. Artistic *gravitas*

Pat live with bouzouki: 'Back to the music within, to the sounds of the heart, of the homeland.'

combined with a disciplined and deeply committed work ethic convinced him that this was a opportunity not to be missed out on. Whether or not it would make money was not really the point at this stage of the game. Pat is unstinting in his praise for Jonathan who not only fitted in with two grieving brothers but soon became like 'the third leg of a stool' musically.

> He was a very, very, very, important member of the Celtus project. Jonathan brought the whole keyboard and programming aspect to Celtus. He was young, he had been to school and he knew what we were looking for. We had all these ideas in our heads and he was transferring them and making them happen.

Jonathan, in return, remembers that even though this was clearly a 'real transitional period' there was a 'spiritual click' with the brothers. It did not matter that he was not a family member, a fellow Irishman, nor indeed experiencing bereavement. As a unit then, rehearsals and recording began in the basement studio until there was something resembling a full album's worth of material which Lindy, now as the new band's sole manager, felt certain could fly commercially.

In the past, when Lindy had gone with John to Denmark Street to buy studio essentials, she had often stood at the junction on Charing Cross road looking up at the EMI Publishing offices. She had read all about Peter Reichardt's Queen's Award in *Music Week* and was only too aware of his reputation as the best, most successful, publisher of the time. Often she would say to herself 'One day I'm going to sign the boys up there. ' Having had the tough experience of the latter years with Mama's Boys, and having seen the thankless slog of touring and recording without label support, she decided that this time she would not mess about with half-measures. Dismissing the interest shown by a small label in the US which offered very little financial security, therefore, she now homed in on one particular address

> I started at the top. I had cards printed as soon as we came up with the name Celtus: a conflation of 'Celt' and 'Us. ' As A&R people do not answer the phone, I turned my attention to a publisher. Directly to the top. To Peter Reichardt, Head of EMI Music Publishing.

Of course Personal Assistants are paid to protect CEOs from unsolicited calls, from hopefuls and their management, and so the real task was not just to get a quality demo to the top man, but to get him to actually listen to it. It was not uncommon for 50 or 60 cassettes a day to arrive in Jiffy bags, only to be swept out, unopened, on Friday afternoon. Lindy, thus, devised an ingenious

Celtus: John, Adam, Pat, Giles and Jonathan.

strategy (endorsed by close friend, and Aerosmith manager, Wendy Laister) which, it transpired, was then coupled with some good luck. In Harrods she bought an elegant mahogany box, had Celtus engraved on the silver lid, then laid out the demo cassette on two bright green silk hankerchiefs, alongside a message written on a calling-card which stated confidently 'With millions of Irish immigrants in America, I think we can sell this. Lindy. ' All of this was then tied with a bow, closed with a wax seal embossed with a large 'C', and delivered personally to the front desk at EMI Publishing where, by pure chance, it turned out to be the CEO's, Peter Reichardt's, birthday. Assuming it to be a present, and quite a pricey one at that, his PA put the box in his present bag with all of the others, gave it to the chauffeur who put it in the car, and drove it home to Peter's wife who, it turned out, was Irish. When he got back from work a few hours later he was taken by such an elegant and eye catching gift from someone he didn't even know, and so opened it and played the cassette, and loved it. He called Lindy immediately and left a message saying 'I think you better come in and see me. ' In the background of this treasured message left on their answering machine, an excited John and Lindy could hear the poignant *Brother's Lament*.

The resultant meeting gave rise to a certain amount of optimism. Though EMI would definitely have to see the band perform live, they would also need a record deal in place in order to commit themselves to anything. That said, Reichardt certainly understood the talent he was dealing with. When Muff Winwood (brother of Stevie), head of Sony, heard the demo tape of *Brothers Lament* and *Moonchild*, and also of Reichardt's interest, he requested the fledgling Celtus, not yet a full band, to do a showcase at Nomis Studios. To take to the stage again, without Tommy behind them, was a Rubicon that the brothers were going to have to cross sooner or later. As they approached the first anniversary of his death there was a real sense that it was now time to get on with life, and music, again if only for his sake. Accordingly, rehearsal studios were booked and paid for, session musicians hired, and over a hundred green invitations mailed out for the three song showpiece.

The event, however, was a fiasco. What nobody had seen coming was that the night before the performance the MTV awards ceremony was held in Paris, attracting virtually everybody in the music business away from London. This grim reality was then exacerbated by a strike at the airports which meant that no-one could get back in time, even if they had made plans to do so. Reichardt himself had been called away to a last-minute meeting in LA, Muff Winwood failed to show, and the rep from Polydor stayed for only half a song. Even though John looks back on the performance and recalls 'I was so relieved it was over. I was nervous taking on new things I had never done before' Lindy remembers the feeling of destitution

> The room was empty and it was very demoralizing. I rang the van hire company and was told it had been blocked in at a university, so it was delayed in collecting us. We sat around chatting, ate the nibbles and started to pack up.

Then, she recalls, out of the jaws of defeat

> Muff Winwood appeared through the door. I jumped up and told him it was over and he gruffly asked if the guys could play two songs. I ran to the stage and told them 'Muff is here, two more songs, quick!' And so they did.

As soon as they finished Muff came up to the stage and said 'I love what you are doing.' John remembered simply 'He was blown away with the band.' At the subsequent meeting at Sony a few days later however he remarked that 'Marketing will be a problem. It's beautiful music but I'm baffled where to place it. It's not The Pogues, it's not Clannad, yet there's rock in there.' He also made a big point about how he, alongside his marketing department, normally saw an act at least three or four times live during a tour before making a final commitment. A re-run showcase was therefore proposed as the absolute minimum in Celtus' case. This involved costs that were just not available however and so when both Peter and Muff chipped in, there came the first indication that Celtus had an excellent chance of being signed. Even though Christmas 1995 was drawing near, and Lindy and John were getting ready to go to Canada, the latter recalls 'I didn't want to go anywhere as I was eager to wait around, in case the phone rings and we're not here, with someone trying to offer us a record deal.' But Christmas passed, the crucial performance eventually happened in early February, and this time it was a 'complete sell out' – jam packed to the rafters. Peter and Muff pushed their way through the crowd and stood right at the front of the stage, while friends and agents were crammed out into the corridor, unable get into the room. It seems that word had got out (and indeed had been carefully manipulated to leak) that EMI was going to sign Celtus, and that now it was just a case of ascertaining which record label (very probably Sony) was going to go along with them. John broke the ice from the stage by thanking everyone for coming to 'Celtus's first sold-out gig' which raised a laugh and masked his own fears about changing from bass to whistle and, once again, taking the limelight. With no bass, he said, it was like 'dancing without a partner. ' Dante Bonutto, long time and fervent supporter of the McManus brothers was also there, observed no such hesitancy or uncertainty, and instead delighted in the fact that, as ever, the McManus boys 'were true to their roots', that they were 'ploughing their own furrow', and were clearly undertaking this musical metamorphosis with the greatest of ease.

The next day a call came from Muff in which he stated 'I liked what I saw yesterday, tell the boys well done, that was excellent, very talented, and I'm interested in moving forward on this. ' Lindy, appreciating that they had done more than their fair share to prove themselves, was ready with her answer and so with a thumping heart said, 'Are you making a formal offer?' He was. Lindy remembers

> I hung up the phone and squealed! We couldn't believe it! John and I just hugged, laughed, cried and jumped up and down in the kitchen for about 10 minutes like big kids. I was so happy for them, at last, an opportunity they so deserved -a brighter future. It was the ultimate panacea.

Immediately Lindy called Pat, then Reichardt, with the good news to which the latter replied 'I thought you would. So, you used to stand outside looking up to my office determined to get your boys signed did you? Now we have to get this show on the road. ' Lindy still regards getting Celtus from nowhere to signed with Sony / EMI as 'one of the proudest moments -after seven years hard slog, against the cultural flow of the musical tide, getting a dropped band re-signed and within a year of Tommy's death. ' John agrees and acknowledges 'After everything we had been through, after such a bout of awful luck, in such a short period of time, here we were getting presented with something incredibly special ... a future. '

As far as the marketing gurus were concerned too, this was a combination that had a real chance of success, especially as U2 and Riverdance had already blazed a trail for all things Irish across the world before them. From this path-finding Celtus, and the emergent Corrs, could only benefit (John is quick to point out that *Moonchild* was actually started before the whole Riverdance phenomenon took off, and if anything, was rather eclipsed by it). Roderick O'Connor went further in an article called 'Flying the Celtic Flag', seeing the entire project as a marketing executive's dream: the name Celtus, the type of music, the attitude and competence of the artists, the musical pedigree behind 'atmospheric, ethereal and wistful' music that was bound to appeal to 'the crystal gazing New Age hippy in you. ' Warily however, he navigated a route around the name itself saying 'Celtic now has

John on the whistle: 'I have written this piece of music and I would really like it if I could play it for you.'

associations with the best of cultural output as well as dubious marketing ploys which devalue the word. 'This, they were being warned, would have to be handled expertly from the outset. If not, the band, the music and their careers, would be relegated to the realms of kitsch from day one. Dante Bonutto had no such fears and observed that 'Irish culture is incredibly nostalgic and attractive to people. Myth and history become one in Ireland, and that is recognized internationally. ' Such a legacy was perfectly safe in the McManus brothers' hands.

If being signed to the biggest record label and publishing house in the world was not an auspicious enough start, Celtus' live debut was at the Royal Albert Hall supporting Sheryl Crow. Any cautious idea of 'lets start off slowly and see where we go from there' was consigned to the dustbin, especially when the audience reaction was deafening, in stark contrast to Mama's Boys on their first night at the Hexagon in Reading all those years ago. For Jonathan it was doubly daunting as the Albert Hall was in fact his first ever gig as a professional musician in London and, despite suffering from a PA which had been plugged in backwards (resulting in 'farting and popping all over the place,') handled his debut like a seasoned pro. When it was over John joked to Malcolm Rogers 'If they offer us a residency there we'll definitely take it. Nice and handy. Nice audience. ' Rogers rounded off his article with a great compliment, telling his readers that 'you will sit back and say "Ah yes! They do write songs like that anymore". '

John's confidence was coming back too and he recalls 'It felt fantastic to be back at the front of the stage again because this time I knew that I could do it. ' Making a video of every performance and playing it back to work on improvements, he allowed himself to admit

> I was beginning to come into my own as a singer. I had a new found confidence at that stage, a new instrument, new potential, new direction and with the addition of computers, new possibilities. I felt I had loads of things to offer.

One reviewer, Claire Hamill, agreed fully, writing 'but it is the voice of John McManus that stops you in your tracks. ' Another said that they could not fail 'with John McManus having a voice made in heaven that fits where they come from like a glove. ' Sheryl Crow herself, when she heard the broad musical palette and textures, remarked 'Those harmonies are just amazing. '

Getting into the studio to record a proper album was now a priority, so in September 1996 Celtus went into Metropolis for Sony. There were brand new compositions to work with, new 'soundscapes' that spoke of fusion in a way that Mama's Boys had never done, a decent budget, and experts with whom to develop every conceivable idea. The home videos shot in these recording sessions show an arsenal of instruments, including the uilleann pipes, bodhrán, fiddle, bousouki, tin whistle, low whistle, and drums of all shapes and sizes. The producer was Rupert Hine who had previously worked with Rush, Tina Turner and Clannad, and some drum parts were tackled by Ray Fean (from Riverdance) and Jean-Michel Biger. As it turned out Rupert Hine didn't have all that much to do as the demos made in the basement had been done more or less perfectly first time round. An expert tweak here, an overdub there, to bring all of the subsonic keyboards, echoing, multi-tracking and haunting vocal harmonies into line -and that just about did it. What Hine *could* offer was personal introductions to legends such as bass players Pino Palladino and Nicolas Fiszman. Talking of the former in particular John remembers 'I promise you it was just unbelievable to watch the guy play. There was a fantastic vibe in the studio and we just let him do whatever he felt. ' Pat goes on 'Pino told us he had never been given such a free hand for a bass part and just went for it. ' He then says that as a result of so many innovative ideas they were left with the tricky problem of what to leave out. Pat reiterates the role of the less known musicians too, especially Jonathan Czerwik, saying 'He was a major, major contributor to that album. Without Jonathan's help I don't think it would be half the album in all honesty. ' Additionally, Giles McCormick on bass and Adam Bushell on drums were auditioned and recruited to get the recording done and, in time, to take the show on the road.

Tonya Henderson of the *Irish World* was sent to interview the band at the studios as *Moonchild* was being recorded. She began her article lightly, by retracing the story of the brothers and their music to the 1980s when the 'good sisters' of The Convent of Mercy in Enniskillen had been plagued by an epidemic of graffiti on the desks, bags, school books and walls, cryptically proclaiming 'Mama's Boys. ' This, it had soon emerged, was a local rock band, which now, mercifully, had morphed into Celtus and an altogether more palatable type of music. John explained to Henderson the importance of the transition, saying that after Tommy's death they had been 'drawn back to the music within, to the sounds of the heart, of the homeland', creating, in the journalist's mind both a 'calm and a longing. ' Henderson could appreciate, especially when perusing the lyrics, that the compositions were rooted in sentiments that invited the listener to 'Look into the dark and endless sky and hear the clouds of crying angels sigh. ' In another interview with VH1 John also spoke a little bit about the music and its relationship to Tommy, saying 'He would have been devastated if we hadn't continued. We had to. ' He reiterated that Tommy would have adored Celtus and confided that he was present in every aspect of the project: the name *Moonchild* was of course him, *Brother's Lament* took its place on the play list, the voice on *Love Turns to Dust* was Tommy's, and the album itself was dedicated to his memory. Pat tried to stay up beat and even attempted to lighten the mood, saying

> He had 28 glorious years. He was a man who really enjoyed himself. He was ill from he was very young and carried that through his entire music career. We used to tell him to slow down a bit and not to tempt fate. He'd say 'Ah sure I mightn't be here that long. ' He would be standing in the middle of his suitcase at four o'clock in the morning, saying 'I'm going to a club', even if we were in the back of beyond.

John also tried to keep it light in the same interview saying 'We remember more of the good times and the years we had with him rather than what it was like towards the end. It's better not to dwell too much on that. ' Pat reiterated this, even if his attempts to cover his feelings were transparent, when he said 'Tommy packed more into a decade than most people will in a lifetime, and that isn't something to be sad about. '

But there was plenty to be sad about in these tunes and some argued Tommy's spirit ran through every composition as 'haunting melodies cascade out of the speakers like waves crashing against some desolate cliff.' Pat claimed only that 'We play what we feel from our heart, ' while John stated more specifically that 'Tommy's been steering the ship from above.' Putting the two facts together *The Sunday World* printed an article called 'Out of the Celtic Twilight' in which it was said that Tommy's death may have 'folded the band and [caused their] retreat[ed] into limbo', but it had also led to a hitherto unimaginable 'blend of traditional feel and contemporary sounds. ' Elsewhere its complexity was identified as 'Glowering, moody rock music, polished and textured, earthed with the ethnic sound of Irish trad. ' Paul Sexton of the *Times* also got close when he talked of 'dreamy sonic panoramas' which combined 'the soaring power of Clannad, the atmosphere of Enya, and some of those dark passages that surface with Pink Floyd. ' Steve Caseman's review of *Moonchild* reveled in 'a sensitively worked album with a strong attraction, boasting faint eastern flavorings and a contemporary use of rhythm, ' then finished with one word: 'Intriguing. ' When Pat was asked to describe their new direction he made reference to 'Pictures of Landscape' in which there was 'a culmination of contemporary sounds focusing on big, deep, pensive rock rather than a straight ethnic vibe. ' The management concurred describing it as 'Pink Floyd meets Clannad meets Enigma. '

The lyrics too came across as poetic and personal. The words, like the notes, gravitated towards the spiritual, ruminating on the triumph of good over evil, of love over hate, and life over death. There was one more difference too, and Pat told Damien Murray of the *Irish News* in the report 'Group on First Step of Fame Ladder' what it was. Though they were back as musicians and as performers, this time it was purely for the love of the music and nothing else. John Walshe from *Hot Press* was relieved, recalling that the traditional element had never really died over the years anyway, even in the dressing room at Mama's Boys gigs where the boys could be found belting out reels and jigs as they waited to take the stage. One overawed, if slightly frustrated, critic wrote 'Describing the music on Celtus' debut LP *Moonchild* as reels and jigs is like describing Maradonna as a bit of a footballer.' As far as possible from Irish kitsch, Colm O'Hare hallmarked the emotive *Moonchild* 'As good an example of post-modern traditional fusion as you'll get – and better than most.' Veteran Horslips bassist Barry Devlin marveled at the dual handling of both personal and Celtic imagery, and declared it all to be in 'phenomenally good taste.'

This music was being taken very seriously indeed and to the boys it all felt so much more comfortable, genuine and real, coming as it did from the legacy of Big John and Valerie. John acknowledged

> the love that was embedded into [us] for music came from our parents and the local musicians from around home. We were probably brought into the world to the sound of a fiddle playing in the corner somewhere.

Music had always been an international language of communication, something they had known for years but perhaps had had to push to the back of their minds in the days of Mama's Boys when the mighty dollar attempted to take precedence. In John's memory the farmhouse in Fermanagh had always been full of French and Germans playing away with the locals, communicating perfectly without uttering a word. Celtus was a return to that borderless magic and represented a clean break from Mama's Boys, the era and the genre. Pat remembers the welcome return to familiarity.

> When Celtus came along it was *Strange Days in the Country*, which was so much easier to write about. It was a better medium for me as it was coming from an Irish feel. All I'd ever heard about growing up was the ancient race, the old ways, the old people and the old tunes. So it was easy for me to immerse myself in that.

Celtus at The Borderline: 'Glowering, moody rock music, polished and textured, earthed with the ethnic sound of Irish trad.'

Pat live with violin and guitar: 'As good an example of post-modern traditional fusion as you'll get, and better than most.'

Perhaps the real acid test came when they hit the stage to promote *Moonchild*. Allie White of *The Irish World* saw them on November 28 1997 at the Shepherd's Bush Empire and observed that unlike the spectacular days of Mama's Boys there was now no fuss, no explosions and no dry ice. Instead there was a lone low whistle 'to musically caress their audience, to invite them into a mystical, Celtic world. ' Under a single spotlight, centre stage, John epitomized 'a poignant loneliness, a temperate state' which soon passed and was replaced with the ever-present feeling of contentment and devotion to music. No egos, no one-upmanship, only the sharing of an art amongst those who knew how to appreciate it and who experienced its perfect reproduction live. White signed off with 'I can only say, if you don't experience them at least once in your life, you've really missed out. ' The BBC had already taken heed and recorded the whole show for future airing on Radio 2.

As an acknowledgement of her contribution to the eye-catching and ongoing success of Celtus, Lindy was awarded the Young Manager of the Year Award at the Music Managers Forum in 1997. This was a plush affair held at the Hilton in Park Lane in front of hundreds of music industry attendees, and although a founder member of the organization she had almost given the evening a miss. Convinced to go only at the last minute, and seated at the top table, she heard the presenter say something about 'brothers from Northern Ireland' while simultaneously on screens around the room the album cover for *Moonchild* appeared. Next the title track began to play and before she knew it she was on the stage receiving her certificate, a cheque, and a year's free band insurance. She remembers

> It was totally unexpected. I was so touched I could hardly talk. I just wished John had been there. I thanked the MMF for their valuable support and also thanked Tommy, up above. With Gail Colson who had just won Manager of the Year for her work with The Pretenders, Terence Trent D'Arby, Peter Gabriel, and Nigel Kennedy, we were both together in *Music Week* and *Billboard* which gave me terrific networking access.

When she and John got married in 1996 she kept such hard-earned momentum alive by retaining her maiden name instead of changing and attracting remarks about nepotism. It made business sense too, at least on the surface of it all, to create a little distance between business and close-knit family, and meant that feedback on the band tended to be much more unbiased.

Next, hot on the heels of her award came a further compliment when Celtus received a huge international endorsement at the 4th Irish World

Awards '98 at The Galtymore Ballroom in Cricklewood Broadway. Attended by some 1300 people in what could broadly be described as Ireland's answer to the 'Brits', Celtus stormed to victory with *Moonchild* being awarded the Phil Lynott Memorial 'Best Album' Award. Presented by Philomena Lynott, Phil's mum, Pat and John knew that they had seen off The Corrs, Enya and U2 to win this. They also knew that, once again, like it or not, they were back in the big league. Pat kept his feet on the ground though and told a TV interviewer 'We were amazed and astonished that we were even in the running for it.' Privately, unable to shake off the cynicism brought about by earlier dealings with the music industry, he later admitted.

> To me it was all superficial stuff where there were people trying to gain something from it. It is water off a duck's back to me. It was lovely, don't get me wrong, but 'so what?' It doesn't mean anything.

Jonathan Czerwik does not dismiss it so easily and remembers thinking to himself 'You guys really deserve this after such a tough time in the business and personally.'

The first single chosen by the Sony team was *Every Step Of The Way* and was released on January 12 1998 (with *Loch Brann* -a 400 year old traditional Irish tune that their grandmother used to sing to them -on the b-side). Perhaps it was here that a vaguely familiar, scarcely perceptible, unease began to set in again. In the same way that a record plugger can't approach a radio station without finished recorded tracks, the same thing applies for the TV, and videos. Therefore, with only very vague consultation and no clear direction artistically from Sony, a staggering £40,000 of the label's money was allocated for a video shoot in Ireland (with an entire film crew holed up in a pricey hotel owned by Bono). The project was in the safe hands of the same Director of Marketing who had picked up ten nominations and four MTV awards for his work on Jamiroquai's *Virtual Insanity* which in itself had shot to a very respectable number 3 in the charts. John remembers the lurking suspicion however, that for all they were in the hands of seasoned professionals they were also losing control artistically, saying 'All we had said from the beginning was that we didn't want a video that made us look like an Irish group. We didn't want pubs and Guinness. But that is exactly what we ended up with.' From scene to scene the progression was predictable: a red haired girl running, a meadow, a village, a farmer, green fields and Pat and John at the centre of this retro period piece dressed in long coats. The finished result did not entirely please Reichardt either who suggested to Muff that sections of it be re-shot and

CELTUS

Celtus: 'Weaving a strong thread of magic.'

asked that the boys' image be tweaked a bit further. It was important to keep them as young looking as possible, and more 'new-age' than 'folk.' The shoot also came with its light moments. Pat laughs when he remembers the faces of the English crew when, during an attempt to create all things Irish, an 'old geezer on a bicycle cycled through the set with a lump of bailer twine about 10 feet long out behind him and a little dog tied trotting along behind.' It was perfect, and it was, unlike the rest of the storyboard, genuine. Also, the Garda station in the village seemed to be permanently closed, though it did have a note up on the door saying that if anyone had anything important to report, or any gripes, they could come back between two and five. If the record company had wanted Ireland they had got it. They really didn't have to create it.

Having been pushed into a theme, and having had most of their ideas ignored, mainstream TV didn't pick up on the video anyway. MTV and VH1 were consistently inundated with new videos and could only open up between six and ten slots a week. Celtus did not secure one of those slots. In fact, John reckons 'It was only me and my family that ended up seeing this work that had just cost a whole shit load of money.' Lindy fumed at the cost and the lack of accountability for where, specifically, it had all gone. At the back of her mind she also began to acknowledge the reality that Celtus was indeed a very difficult brand to market, and was relieved to see both the German and New Zealand markets open up. Soon they would tour and this, coupled with glowing critical reviews, might help them notch up the 30,000 sales (or get them the hit single) they needed to pay back their Advances, after which they would be in the clear. Pat believed, utterly, that the road was where they would truly excel and viewed the alternative use of money as a strategic error.

> We should have taken whatever money Sony came up with and bought a big van, a big PA, and got out and played every theatre up and down England and Europe and anywhere else, and we could have been really big because it was working. Make no mistake about it.

But Muff Winwood had ruled that out entirely from the beginning, saying that Sony had no budget for such expenses. And though he had emphasized 'You are not in the 100 metres sprint', he had his bosses too, most of whom wanted to see make-it-or-break-it results within a year. After all, *Moonchild* had set Sony back in the region of £500,000 in Advances, recording and touring, and so when everything was totted up, Celtus was costing (not making) the label thousands of pounds a week. Pat certainly remembers the powers that be 'taking one look at us' and asking 'What are the returns on this band?', reminding him of what he had seen once before at Jive. In the meantime though they had all become proficient at wearing the mask and giving super-positive interviews that exposed none of these cracks or doubts. When sales figures and critical reviews started to come in Pat commented humbly 'It's remarkable that so many people liked it. ' But like it the British audiences did, and so the brothers began to long to get further afield – perhaps to the US where there was as yet no release. John remembers with palpable frustration that the entire US market had already been tried out with Mama's Boys and that it was a sure fire thing that 'the audience would just go mental for it. 'Why couldn't they 'land us in New York on St. Patrick's Day and watch what happens next?' Why couldn't the record company have kept Celtus on the festival circuit or at a succession of fashionable ethnic music gatherings which would have allowed them to ride the same Irish wave as Riverdance had done? Pat singles out, in addition to the Chicago and Milwaukee Fests, the notion that Brittany and other regions of France would have also been culturally compatible. That said, he also concedes, there would have been no point in even asking for these foreign excursions as 'Sony would have said "Look lads, if you can't get this away in your own country, how the hell are you going to get it away in America?"' Dan Axtell, soon to be keyboards player in Celtus after Jonathan's departure, agreed and argued that as Celtus' music 'was in the vein of Moby, and not purely Irish, it should not have been dependent on America for success. ' In any case, the record company said 'no' to such an expensive jaunt, having had their fingers burned in a similar manner with Kula Shaker, and so left in its place only a long list of 'what ifs. ' In the meantime, if Celtus shifted thousands of CDs, if they got some serious radio and TV exposure in the UK, or if they made some significant impact with film scores and soundtracks, *then* the US might be worth the gamble, but not until there was a rock solid financial reason for doing it.

When Celtus did play live, it was memorable. In the UK their star remained undoubtedly in the ascendant and soon they did a show, and interview, for VH1 at The Borderline where they were almost regulars. Big John, now in his 70s, was there cheering his boys on, as was world boxing champion Barry McGuigan and his wife Sandra. In fact, McGuigan went on to use *Brother's Lament* for his television boxing show *Ringside*, perhaps because he could empathize with the McManus boys, not only as his father had known them years ago, but as his own daughter had Leukaemia. Later he wrote of both their talent and personalities, saying

They have a unique sound; think Kate Bush amalgamated with the Clannad melodies and you get the inimitable sound that the McManus boys make. They are exceptionally talented musicians and humble down-to-earth with it, which is a very refreshing virtue these days.

In July Celtus climbed even higher and played the main stage of the WOMAD Festival at Reading in front of over 17,000 people. This was the World Organization of Music and Dance which Peter Gabriel had set up years before to promote ethnic music, dance, art and food. It was a nice cultural mix and perhaps a little bit more sophisticated than the rock festivals of years gone by. At least no-one was flinging mud this time. On a fine day, selling hundreds of CDs from the festival merchandiser, winning over thousands of new fans who had not even known the name Celtus when they arrived, the boys impressed everybody. Muff had even started bringing boxes of promo CDs to concerts, despite company policy to the contrary, as he was aware that this way the music was getting directly to those who appreciated it the most. Celtus then performed at the Celtic Rock Festival at the Quays in Galway and this was filmed by RTE. Ethereal, atmospheric, emotional, complex and original: every note was replicated perfectly with almost studio precision. John and Pat certainly seemed to be back in their realm. When the bodhrán started the tribal beat kicked up a storm that Tommy would have adored. At times the old rocker in Pat was let loose on his guitar too and this served as a reminder of why he had always been considered such a maestro. As a band, or as a collective of talented individuals, Celtus proved that the McManus brothers had dusted themselves down and reinvented themselves. In short, they were back.

Chapter 8: *Portrait* and After:

Behind all of the critical acclaim, the positive press reviews, the enthusiastic audience reception at venues like the Royal Albert Hall, and the fast-growing fan club (which now had over 3000 members worldwide), there was a serious problem. *Moonchild* was not selling fast enough to offset the money the band had cost the label, nor was it even pushing them significantly closer to re-paying the Advances. There was clearly nothing wrong with the music, and there was certainly no complaint about the commitment or proficiency of the band and its management, but sales were struggling to rise above the 8000 mark. And here lay the supreme irony for the eleven-strong corporate team involved in the Celtus project. A conundrum had been brought about by the originality of the music which, with no direct precedent, could not really be labeled, or placed into any readily identifiable or pre-existing category. For example, in a high street outlet like HMV, in which section would you look for Celtus: Rock / Ethnic / World / Irish / Folk? Original keyboardist Jonathan Czerwik looks back and concludes that, after all, perhaps this was 'the wrong label to be with' and that perhaps a smaller company might have had more time and vested interest in pushing the band in all the right places. In any case, he sums up, a multi-national such as 'Sony was a strange place for Celtus to be. ' No-one denied for a second the tremendous advantages of great studios, impressive first gigs, tours and steady Advances, but beyond that there was an over-riding feeling that Celtus was drifting rather than being steered. Understanding the seriousness of the problem Muff Winwood went so far as suggesting a name change for the band, though Lindy and Peter Reichardt vetoed this, feeling that it would lead to a loss of hard-earned momentum. John identified the same problem, saying 'The name Celtus was causing us problems as when we said it people thought of The Dubliners. ' Pat, on the other hand, while acknowledging some truth in the diagnosis, refuses to let it get out of proportion

That really is looking for excuses when you try to blame failure, or lack of success, on a name. Blame the name. If it's successful people don't care what the name is. We had this argument with Mama's Boys too. They said rockers would never wear a T-shirt with 'Mama's Boys' on it.

The marketing people at the label were not all convinced that the name was a problem either as they were making great progress with Jamiroquai – an unconventional name to say the least. And anyway, what would be a better alternative to 'Celtus'? To compound the disorientation, and to further evade definition, the new demos created in preparation for the *Portrait* album had been planned from the beginning to mark a shift away from the *Moonchild* style into something more experimental. John had already told Gareth Gorman of *Living Abroad Magazine* to expect the end of the distinctively Irish sound and to get ready for a move away from those instruments in favor of further innovation and originality. *Moonchild* (or 'The Tommy Album' as Pat called it) had served its purpose: it had escorted the brothers through dark days and it had got them re-signed. Now it was time to move on. Perpetual reinvention was healthy and an integral ingredient in keeping the talented five-piece fresh and original, but it was wreaking havoc with marketing executives who had only just got their heads around what the first album had brought to the table. Accordingly, a break in the ranks was beginning to show within the label about the wisdom of committing more money to a second album. Muff successfully convinced Sony Chairman Paul Burger that Celtus were so very close to major success now that it would be a crime to walk away, then privately expressed deep concern to the band that there really had to be a hit this time. He hinted strongly that it was now or never.

Full label support, in the form of another £500,000, was dutifully allocated for the recording of *Portrait* and no corners cut in producing a world class follow up to the debut. Indeed, such was the level of corporate commitment that stylists were even employed to give the boys new haircuts and re-jig their wardrobes, experts were brought in to discuss the colors used for the upcoming album sleeve, and a list of Grade A studios made available for the work to come. Two tracks, *The Awakening* and *Cathedral*, were actually recorded at the legendary Abbey Road Studios. Pat, John and Jonathan, were immediately entranced by the history of the place, the pedigree of the musicians who had recorded there, and of 'the classics' whose genesis had been realized within these walls. In true Spinal Tap manner Pat picks up the story

> We were standing in the room where the Beatles had recorded so much. John and I were in the room looking around and John says 'Can you feel the vibes here? Just think, in that very corner John Lennon sat. ' And I said 'Yeah! Incredible!' 'And Paul McCartney was over there, and Ringo was over there. Man you can just hear it echo round the room. '

Rooted to the spot and in awe of the musical adventure that had taken them from the farmhouse in Fermanagh to this Mecca, the mood was suddenly broken when the intercom crackled and someone at the mixing desk, who had been eavesdropping, hit the talk-back button and said 'Boys, you're in the wrong room for all that.' Pat winds up the embarrassing story with 'We sidled off quick.' Beatles or no Beatles it was nevertheless magical for Pat to hear his own compositions transcribed in full and played by a sixteen piece orchestra conducted by Gavyn Wright a few days later. The services of a hip producer, Matthew Vaughan, who had previously been associated with The Verve, and later Mike and the Mechanics, were also called in. Vaughan was, in Pat's recollections, 'a whizz kid' with an untouchable knowledge of dance beats, drum loops and programming, and perhaps it was this that made Sony feel sure that this time they had hit upon the illusive recipe for success.

A hit single was needed and this had always been Pat's nemesis. He knew that a catchy tune could turn the band's fortunes around, break them through conclusively to the success that remained so tantalizingly close, and perhaps land them a renewed deal for a third album. Even though he really wanted to pursue his interests in the 'Darker, new world, ethnic feel music', instead he sat down to write something that he thought would sell. That same old sinking feeling returned, that if their careers, once again, were hanging on his writing a toe-tapping three minute single, they were indeed on thin ice. This was not what Celtus was about, it never had been. They were not an MTV act, but frustratingly no-one was heeding this. They needed to be aimed at a more mature, sophisticated clientele. Pat reflects with more than a hint of fatalism on the decisions taken in those days, and how with such prerequisites they were always going to be fighting against the odds

> I knew it wasn't going to happen right from the word go. I knew on *Moonchild* that it wasn't going to happen. From the first three weeks of that album being finished I knew. I knew it in my heart but I didn't tell anybody. The record company was going right down the wrong road because that is not what we were about. We were lucky to get a second album at all.

His frustration was compounded by the blinding fact that the *cognoscenti* so widely understood, indeed applauded, Celtus' focus on complex, multi-layered music and its inimitable texture. And yet the barometer of success within the industry remained intransigently on whether or not they could come up with something that could be neatly packaged and put onto the radio and TV, then sold by the thousand to teenagers. John remembers the

October 1999

Sat 9th	**LIVERPOOL ROYAL COURT**	
	Tel: 0151 709 4321 / 2	
Mon 11th	**YORK BARBICAN**	
	Tel: 01904 656688	
Tues 12th	**BIRMINGHAM SYMPHONY HÀLL**	
	Tel: 0121 212 3333	
Thurs 14th	**NOTTINGHAM ROYAL CONCERT HALL**	
	Tel: 0115 948 2626 / 948 2525	
Sun 17th	**MANCHESTER PALACE THEATRE**	
	Tel: 0161 242 2550	
Wed 21st	**SHEFFIELD CITY HALL**	
	Tel: 01142 789789 / 565656	
Thurs 22nd	**NEWCASTLE CITY HALL**	
	Tel: 0191 261 2606	

Tickets available from venues and all usual agents (subject to booking fee).
24 HOUR CREDIT CARD HOTLINE TEL: 0115 912 9129 (All venues)
(subject to booking fee).
For lowest booking fees - buy online and save at www.ticketweb.co.uk.
Or by phone on 0171 771 2000.

Deacon Blue Tour: 'There is very little that overawes them.'

all-too-familiar scene well, saying 'By the time *Portrait* was being worked on we were scrambling around in the dark again, not really staying true to our own beliefs … trying to please someone else.' He went on to say that it had rapidly become 'another act of desperation. Everything was geared towards the record company again, except for the bits where we were ourselves, and so the album was a bit disjointed.' When asked about writing the actual 'hit-single' Pat interrupts with obvious residual frustration 'Yes, yes, but that was me trying to write a song which was marketable, but something that I didn't really believe in either.'

Whether he believed in it or not, the syncopated *Wide Awake* was that single, and was as catchy as could be. Surely this would sell, not least as the video had been made by the same top-dollar S2 team, headed by Adolfo Doring, who had recently done the celebrated Bon Jovi videos. The record company really must have believed in Celtus after all, especially as the pricey *Every Step of the Way* had not been aired widely on TV at all. On location on Camber Sands, near Rye, where Coldplay had done their recent video, John took centre stage in a production that was, in all fairness, very well done. The second section of the shoot featured John, Pat, Jonathan, Giles and Adam, and was filmed at a depot in Kings Cross where strobe lights, heaps of equipment and bonfires dominated the night scene, and reminded the viewer of the unmistakable truth that this fresh new incarnation of Celtus was as a rock band. The song sounded good, the band looked good, Radio 2 picked up on it and the single came into the charts at a very respectable number 39. Angela Rippon and Terry Wogan plugged it a lot, to the point that the breakthrough this time seemed assured. And then, just as quickly as hope had been raised, it was dashed again, as the song faded away and out of the charts the following week.

As the principal writer, and as an artist dedicated to the importance of both words and notes, Pat was only concerned about the charts because other people were relying on him. It was, in his opinion, a poor substitute for good music, for communication, at a time when he was interested in presenting a more mature set of meditations on life. The album's title track *Portrait*, for example, was a majestic song, motivated by the same impetus that had inspired him to pen both *Belfast City Blues* and *Freedom Fighters* so many years ago. How inconceivable, how ludicrous, that the same 'Troubles' were still being bitterly thrashed out all these years later: still costing lives, still mired down in stalemate, still based on a fictional set of identities that drove apart otherwise peaceful communities. In *Freedom Fighters* he had asked 'The smoke it ascends high into the sky / Mission complete, beneath the ashes their lies / Broken hearts and empty homes / When will they

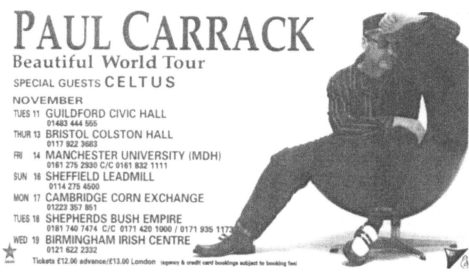

PAUL CARRACK
Beautiful World Tour
SPECIAL GUESTS **C E L T U S**

NOVEMBER
TUES 11 GUILDFORD CIVIC HALL
01483 444 555
THUR 13 BRISTOL COLSTON HALL
0117 922 3683
FRI 14 MANCHESTER UNIVERSITY (MDH)
0161 275 2930 C/C 0161 832 1111
SUN 16 SHEFFIELD LEADMILL
0114 275 4500
MON 17 CAMBRIDGE CORN EXCHANGE
01223 357 851
TUES 18 SHEPHERDS BUSH EMPIRE
0181 740 7474 C/C 0171 420 1000 / 0171 935 1173
WED 19 BIRMINGHAM IRISH CENTRE
0121 622 2332
Tickets £12.00 advance/£13.00 London (agency & credit card bookings subject to booking fee)

Paul Carrack Tour: 'Celtus will be doing this when they are fifty.'

'Celtus are quite simply the best band Ireland has ever produced.'

learn just to leave us alone?' Now, all these years later, he was still compelled to address the subject in *Portrait* with the words: 'So give us love and understanding / Give us hope that's never ending / And to the faithful now departed / May you rest in peace, may you never be forgotten / And to the children of tomorrow / May the final act and triumph of our will / Be your walk to freedom.' In the meantime the reality, exacerbated by the horrors of the Omagh bomb, was grim, and so he despaired

> how pointless all of it is. The families that are left behind to suffer in their day-to-day living. Nobody understands the suffering. Pictures on a mantelpiece, faces gone, lost to mindless violence. I was trying to put something I understood into a song format.

The brothers had known their own excruciating family losses and could see no possible justification for imposing such heartbreak upon others. Valerie had died in a horrible car accident. Tommy had gone because he had an incurable disease. But to knowingly set out to burden a family with such pain, to willfully break hearts in the name of an ideology, was unforgivable. Avoiding any temptation to be drawn into romantic and patriotic stereotypes therefore, Pat dismissed what he had grown up with, saying

> I have no belief in any of that. I don't think any country, or religion, is worth one drop of blood. I take people at face value. If I like them I like them, if I don't I don't, and it does not matter to me what religion, what creed, what color they are. And that is my final word on it.

John and Pat, through their travels and personal experiences, had had a chance to see and experience many different belief systems, and had subsequently arrived at their own personal philosophies. These were predominantly apolitical in outlook, keen to advocate tolerance not division, and propound individualism over collective identity. Pat remembers being a bit suspicious of the whole organized religion thing even from very early on in life, suspecting then that it may, on the whole, be a shallow form of social control. The three brothers had never really set out to be inappropriate or offensive, and they certainly had never intended to launch any form of attack on the church, but they couldn't help but feel that clergy seemed to preach a lack of tolerance rather than fostering it, and more than anything, seemed to exist through an unthinking ritual that one simply had to get through mechanically every Sunday morning. Coming back from distant gigs in places like Cork, the brothers, as teenagers, would arrive in Derrylin at about the time of first mass, and would dutifully say to each other

New keyboard player Dan Axtell: 'Man could we kick up a storm. All this mad Irish music with mental drum loops…it was fantastic. '

Shall we pull in and get this over and done with? We used to nod off, sitting there in our leather jackets. And people would say 'Oh them Mac lads, they're drugged up to the eye balls.' We were just sleepy.

The artificial division between Protestant and Catholic had also been drilled home on the tour with Hawkwind when, on the Sunday after the Hammersmith Odeon show, like good well-brought-up Fermanagh boys, they decided to get up and go to Mass. Having found a nearby place of worship, and having got half way through the service, they slowly began to realize that they had mistakenly walked into a Church of England. Pat remembers, with humor, that it was Tommy who twigged first and poked him, whispering 'We're in the wrong place.' The sinking feeling that followed was soon replaced by an over-riding sense that 'there was damn all difference.' The temporary amusement that this mistake brought about was soon followed by the absurd realization that this was what people were dying for at home. And so, at the height of 'The Troubles', the McManus boys had steered the neutral path and adopted a moral high ground. Pat recalls today, as he did then, that this was a responsibility, a duty.

We took great pride in going to Belfast and all those people would gather for our shows, Catholics and Protestants. We were all rockers, we were all united, shouting *Straight Forward* (they would then kick the shit out of each other outside). Maybe that was our biggest achievement of all.

Campaigning for peace through the medium of music was as close as the boys had ever got to politics and so Pat, speaking about *Portrait*, told Radio Derby

The situation in Omagh had brought it on – the senselessness of what happened. On one side there is a family grieving and outside there's someone making promises that they'll never keep, and trying to cause more trouble. They never deal with how the families are left in the end to grieve and it's been going on too long. In this day and age, coming into the new millennium, it's got to stop.

Accordingly the parochial, and often intransigent, nature of organized religion as preached in the rural districts of Ireland came in for its share of criticism in emotive songs like *Cathedral*. In this, God talks down to his people through a microphone, through the voice of well-versed preachers, some of whom were simultaneously concealing abominable activities with minors.

And yet, people dogmatically continued to believe, continued dutifully to go to church, continued to support the institution unquestioningly, even when it no longer came naturally or instinctively to do so. For Pat the juxtaposition of paralyzing indifference and institutionalized ritual was captured in the line 'Wake me up in time for midnight Mass.'

Amongst musical connoisseurs *Portrait* was greeted with overwhelming enthusiasm. *The Irish World* spoke for many announcing 'Celtus release wake-up call' then asked why it should be a surprise to watch talented musicians grow, experiment and diversify, especially with talent at their finger tips and a world renowned record company to foster every ounce of their creativity. Next, a good chance emerged for Celtus to open for Mike Oldfield on the *Live Then and Now Tour*, starting at the Grand Rex in Paris (the same day *Wide Awake* was to be released), and followed by enormous shows in Wembley, Birmingham NEC and The Point in Dublin. Peter Reichardt and Mike Oldfield's manager had played a round of golf during which Peter recommended Celtus as the support act. This would involve a pay-to-play deal, or a buy-on, which Muff would have to sanction. Reichardt then called Lindy excitedly from the course to break the great news, and immediately plans were put into motion to get Celtus ready for their biggest gigs yet and the first ever outside the UK. A few weeks later, however, Oldfield and his manager terminated their working relationship abruptly leaving a new management in place which felt little of no obligation to honor old commitments. When Lindy called to ask what was going on she got the jobsworth answer that 'No-one told us about it. It's nothing to do with me.' The disappointment of losing such high profile gigs was soon replaced with the hope that another touring slot might yet open up, this time with Jethro Tull. But again, despite Ian Anderson's personal admiration for the group and their music, his tour went ahead with no support act at all. What did materialize though was a fourteen date tour of the UK with Deacon Blue. Finally, onstage again, Celtus effortlessly found their groove and left one impressed critic at the Royal Albert Hall saying 'after their storming set at last year's WOMAD festival, it would appear that there is very little that over awes them.' The Classic Rock Society reviewed another gig on the same tour at Sheffield City Hall and concluded that there was no way to see this outing as anything other than 'a double header.' Celtus were taking on Deacon Blue and, for sure, holding their own. The reviewer from *Q* Magazine predicted that 'Huge sales and extensive airplay inevitably beckon', and observed the enthusiasm of those waiting at the signings and acoustic sets in HMV, and queuing patiently to buy CDs at the gigs during the short interval. Sometimes as many as 300 promotional CDs a night would shift, just as they had done when they had gone on the road with Paul Carrack. Flogging 'Promotional Use Only' CDs, however profitable and eminently sensible in helping with tour costs, was discouraged as it sidestepped 'the royalty system.' It did however prove beyond any doubt that there was a demand. Muff Winwood, having also seen Celtus get a standing ovation at the London Palladium, told Allie White of *The Irish World* about their long-term future

> I think you'll find that by the third album of Celtus it will be quite different from the first album. I think there'll be less Irish influence and more global influences. Celtus will be doing this when they are fifty. They'll maybe have a slow start but definitely a long fade.

It came as a bit of a surprise then to hear John tell a radio DJ that there might be an element of doubt concerning a third album if sales didn't pick up a bit. This left the interviewer reeling, especially as he had just called *Moonchild* 'the debut album of the 90s.' In fact, by now, a small handful of insiders already knew that the writing was on the wall as far as Sony was concerned. In Pat's recollections Celtus was now doomed by people who 'did not have an ounce of music in them' and who thought about art in terms of selling pieces of plastic. As illogical as it may all have seemed, and as well concealed as the weaknesses were, Celtus were close to spent as a commercial entity. Or at least they soon would be if something didn't improve, fast. Following a high profile performance at the Royal Festival Hall, an appearance on TV with Gloria Hunniford materialized where once again they talked of the international language of music, the influence of Horslips, and the undying support of their family over a lifetime in music. Next came an appearance on the Vanessa Show, some live performances on VH1, a national radio tour with acoustic performances and interviews, and soon there was even talk of performing on the Jools Holland Show. In the latter they were eventually pipped at the post by The Corrs who had just won a Brit Award and were now global. Ex-keyboardist Jonathan called The Corrs and Riverdance 'the kiss of death' for Celtus as they were unbeatable, slick, and multi-national marketing machines. Pat concurs 'The Corrs certainly look the part. It is a marketing persons dream. A family who can do this! There is so much to hang this on.' John laughs about it now saying 'What we really needed was the Corrs to fuck off. I mean these were pretty girls with violins and we looked like left-overs from Iron Maiden.'

In any case, and for whatever reason, it was the end of the road for Celtus and their Sony / EMI relationship. Muff could no longer convince Sony

John: 'A beautiful kaleidoscope of sound.'

Pat: 'I was trying to emulate the sound of the war pipes, the uilleann pipes, especially the rolls and the specific grace notes that those instruments have, and the only way to do it was with two hands.'

UK that the act was worth further investment and this, in conjunction with a major cut in Sony's list of 40 other bands, spelled the end. The relationship was terminated when the contract expired on Christmas Day 1999. Pat looks back charitably enough saying 'I'm not having a go. I don't blame them. They really didn't know what to do with us. 'To many others it seemed nothing short of criminal to be dropped when everything was going so well, when the band had fulfilled every artistic promise it had made at the outset, and when they were just about to set out on a major tour with Jimmy Nail. One critic shrugged it off with disgust saying that this was 'a decision they [Sony] will live to regret. ' Another called it

> one of the most shameful happenings in the music world. Sony dropping Celtus has to be one of the most unethical and unintelligent occurrences that we hope will rebound on them.

Celtus was not the only band to go. Toploader, who had sales of over a million with *Dancing in the Moonlight*, and Reef who had completed a tour with the Rolling Stones, might have felt equally aggrieved. But facts were facts and statistics didn't lie. Downloading had started, the bands were unprofitable, and in the light of Michael Jackson's diminishing sales following child abuse allegations, it was time for Sony to trim their sails for the upcoming year in a music business that was bracing itself for the piracy storm.

Muff was horrified and came round to the house personally to commiserate and ask what he could do to help. But what, in reality, was he going to be able to do? John has nothing but sympathy for him and remembers 'It killed Muff. I really felt for him. The belief he had in this group was unbelievable. It killed him to see it fall apart. ' Muff concluded dolefully

> The music is beautiful, the performances are mesmerizing, the musicianship is superb and the management is great. You are all nice, talented, very hardworking people. But, we have spent 500K on each album, so you have had a million pounds spent on trying to break you. You've had the same push, or possibly more, as any other act. Unfortunately, I can only describe it as this. You can make a beautiful wool coat, with a wonderful silk lining that is almost a work of art. But, if the fashion dictates that everyone is buying cheap plastic macs -the coats won't sell. No matter how beautiful.

Lindy remembers 'I was devastated. It was like another death. Seven years of trying, then three years of struggling. ' Nevertheless, they went out on the 35 date tour which Steve Strange had landed them, and by all accounts it was a phenomenal success. Stripped down to a three-piece format and with nothing whatever to lose now, the audiences in John's memory 'just went ballistic. ' Pat also felt that there was little point in trying to recreate the majestic soundscapes of the *Moonchild* era and so determined to take a different route. He remembers

> We knew that you can't go out there and do all that wishy washy stuff. This is going to die a death if we go out and do that. The old rockers came back out in us and that is where the bodhrán and rhythm sections came from.

Pat, John and new keyboardist Dan Axtell adapted to utilize more computer drum fills, and in so doing beefed up the stage sound in the absence of the original, and expensive, band. Dan remembers 'I loved it. I'm a techno addict. ' John reckons it worked too, and smiles when he recalls 'Man could we kick up a storm. All this mad Irish music with mental drum loops … it was fantastic. ' Critic Paul Brookman cut through all ambiguity in a review of one of these shows to announce impressively 'Celtus are quite simply the best band Ireland has ever produced. ' *Billboard* unreservedly agreed, albeit a bit later, saying 'Celtus has all the potential to be one of the biggest bands to come out of Ireland. ' *Sunday Life*, in an article called 'Brothers in Lore', observed that playing with Jimmy Nail had brought the prodigal McManus brothers back to Belfast (The Waterfront) for the first time since Mama's Boys played the Whitla Hall in 1987. Now they were home again and one day soon, he felt, they would be back as the headline act. But by Christmas 1999 it was clear that if they were to do so it would be on their own dollar.

On the upside, losing the record deal returned artistic freedom to the McManus brothers, while, on the downside, it took away financial security at a time when they needed it the most. Even if they had survived without a label in the past, they could not continue to do so in the future. They had already had two shots at the big time. A third was out of the question. Unsure what else to do other than to carry on, Pat, John and Dan continued their work writing, programming and recording the next album, *Rooted*, which was an existing library commission for Music House/EMI Publishing. Stripped of the big studios, the world famous producers and any other musicians, the album was created in the basement studio, delivered without the slightest interference regarding artistic direction, content and execution, and made available through the Fan Club. By now though Pat had become fatalistic about the whole business side of music making and remembered that he and John would say 'to hell with it, just do it', while all the time knowing that the project was 'a stay of execution.' Of course at the back of both of their minds was the hope that

> Something might happen, like doing the lottery, have a punt. I knew it, John knew it, everyone knew it, but we enjoyed doing it, and we knew if it works out it works out. If it doesn't, we know we gave it a good go.

Probably for these reasons *Rooted* is an interesting album as it offers an insight into what Celtus compositions could sound like when they were free from commercial considerations. Nothing was ever going to get into Top of the Pops anyway, so why try? Pat remembers that that did not mean that making music had become in any way frivolous however

> It was great fun for although we didn't have to think commercially any more for a single we would still invest our heart and soul into it. You could come up with these mad cap ideas and stick something Irishy on top of it, and we'd no time to stop and think about it which was even better. It all seemed to just gel.

It was also probably true to say that Pat's legendary guitarist status had taken back seat for long enough now. Composing for an overall textuality of sound in which the guitar did not dominate (as it had always done in Mama's Boys), the early Celtus compositions had sought an even instrumental blend. Now, however, Pat determined to dig out the guitar again, drag it to the forefront and see what avenues might yet be explored using new experiments and innovative techniques. In inimitable compositions such as *Claddagh: Heart in the Hand* Pat allowed himself to go back to his Irish roots, but through a medium less normally associated with them. He explains

> I was trying the emulate the sound of the war pipes, the uilleann pipes, especially the rolls and the specific grace notes that those instruments have, and the only way to do it was with two hands. To try with triplets and with a traditional plectrum would not have worked. To the best of my knowledge that had never been tried, or achieved, before. I finally managed to get the proper rolls in with the two hands, across more than one string. It was quite complex.

In *Purple Diadem* John and Pat duelled back and forth between guitar and/ or fiddle and whistle 'to give light, and color and shade to the composition.'

'Celtus' by Clive Arrowsmith: 'At last the good ship Celtus has come in.'

What Goes Around *Tour*

All the time though

> In the back of our heads we were thinking that this is a bit like Wishbone Ash musically. I mean *Argus* is old England, old English music, listen to tracks like *Throw Down the Sword* and we had a strong affiliation with all of that.

Ironically *Rooted* actually sold well, certainly enough to offer some very timely encouragement, especially as Lindy had just been approached by the Director of the TV series *Ballykissangel* who was very keen to use Celtus' music for the theme tune. For a whole host of reasons, however, that never happened. To keep Celtus afloat for twelve more months she estimated that a further £150,000 was needed. Though Peter Reichardt and Muff Winwood were still generously doing what they could to help, it was certain that major investors would also be needed. Lindy approached a Venture Capital Investment company, followed the advice of an Oxford Professor, worked on the subsequent Business Plan, and in turn made the lengthy preparations for a make-or-break speech and showcase performance at Ronnie Scotts for 'financial suits.' This coincided with an approach by an independent promoter who felt sure that a headlining tour would be a viable option (based on CD and merchandise sales on the road), kicking off with a London date at the prestigious Queen Elizabeth Hall in March. Though it was undoubtedly difficult to muster up the enthusiasm to keep at it, they all agreed that it was worth a final shot, especially as it would get the new material out to the still-widening fan base. To this plush concert venue 40 music and recording company executives and potential investors were invited, fifteen of whom confirmed attendance immediately. On the night not one showed up, leading Lindy to write in the Fan Club Newsletter 'I suppose it reflects the state of the British Music Industry.' And what a show they missed. If anything, Pat still sees it as the highlight of the band's entire career, boasting 'a light show, video screens, a Pink Floyd feel, with lots of things happening behind the music.' John in particular had made an effort to 'visually give the audience the concept of what we were thinking, as well as the music.' It was 'the way Celtus should be', and nobody who could do anything to help them out saw it. The same was the case when they headlined the Whitchurch Festival which went down a storm, or when they were asked to play at the Classic Rock Society Awards in Rotherham where they shared a stage with the legendary Rick Wakeman. (Pat kept the mood light and told an interviewer 'It'll be "We're not worthy"! I'll be tongue tied, I will! He's more than welcome to play the keyboards. We'll just stand there with our mouths hanging open. ') Thankfully many of these final shows were recorded at different venues and on different occasions by Mat Miller (who later did the Australian Pink Floyd) and subsequently released as *Live 2000*. But with Napster now on the scene, with piracy rife and downloading commonplace, it was fruitless to try and find major label support. Instead, a small, enthusiastic, label called Evangeline Recorded Works emerged and offered to press *Live 2000* and *What Goes Around* for an affordable fee, after which both albums were made available via the website and Fan Club.

In the fifth album, *What Goes Around,* graced with a cover designed by David Axtell (Dan's brother) and bearing a photograph by celebrated photographer Clive Arrowsmith, the experimentation continued, now branching into music from Eastern Europe and Pat's exploration of the ethnic and folk music of Bulgaria. This he observed had very strange time signatures, intriguing scales and fascinating structures, which, when harnessed to his own musical pedigree and innovation, resulted in compositions like the title track and *Jigsaw.* In the latter, an ethnographic approach to music inevitably demanded an appreciation, and then an incorporation, of the history of it -a prospect which enthralled Pat. Every step took him closer to home, to the story telling tradition of music, to the importance of its survival and to the fact, plain and simple, that music was for the people and by the people, not the property of spiritless market forces. He reveled, for example, in the idea that during the Jacobean Rebellion playing music on instruments was forbidden as it was a means of communication. As a result people had to learn to listen carefully, to remember, and to sing music. The only way to pass music on from one person to another then was to sing it, resulting in an entire genre called 'mouth music. ' Hailing from the rural parts of Scotland and the Isles a skilled practitioner could get the correct nuances, inflections and triplets effortlessly in what became known as 'piping. 'When Pat probed a bit deeper he learned that his grandmother had actually taught these techniques. This set him thinking

> maybe there is a way of recording these organic voices and putting them to modern beats. I was actually at home and I heard my father lilting a tune so I switched on my mini disc player. I didn't even tell him. I loved the ambience of the room, the clock ticking in the background. I didn't want a clinical sound. I wanted it to sound old, with a burnt voice, a bad recording. For it to work, it needed that.

Enchanted, Pat took it back and played it to John who looked at him and said 'And what are we going to do with that? Are you mad?' This was a long,

long way from playing *Gentleman Rogues* with Deep Purple at Knebworth, but they got to work anyway and 'had a whale of a time doing it. It was hilarious. ' The result, using a different lilting sample, was the wildly infectious *Jigsaw* which Bill Whelan, the writer of *Riverdance*, told Pat was 'brilliant. ' Pat, in return

> thought to myself, well if I get Bill Whelan's blessing that's good enough for me. I was absolutely chuffed because I really admire him as a musician, a thinker and a producer. There is none better.

One of the only reviews that *What Goes Around* got also singled out *Jigsaw* as a successful attempt to 'take it all onto another plateau' by adding scratching to an already 'juicy musical meal. ' Elsewhere, serious issues were touched upon lyrically in songs like *Angel* which tackled child abuse. Pat recounts that in itself this remained firmly inside the folk tradition, concluding

> It is a modern folk song. Folk singers tell real stories, very seldom they are manufactured in their heads. It is normally about something, a love lost, a death, and this is a modern folk song. They are never really happy.

Shelter explored the war in Afghanistan and closer to home in Northern Ireland (where communities were divided by the width of a street), while *What Goes Around* resigned itself to an over-riding sense that *plus ca change, plus c'est la meme chose.* Though the album represented a dead end commercially, artistically and creatively the band was now stretching itself in ways previously unthinkable. Exuding a middle eastern flavor, regional rhythm structures, and employing whistles, pipes, bodhrán, bouzouki, guitars, fiddles, samples of jazz, some folk and an occasionally computer generated 'ambience', this was a connoisseurs album. One critic described it as 'a beautiful kaleidoscope of sound' and Andrew Judge was similarly won over declaring with finality 'It is a great achievement finally knowing you've got there', before concluding 'at last the good ship Celtus has come in. '

When the carefully prepared Venture Capital showcase at Ronnie Scott's happened, it seemed that Andrew Judge's prediction might just have been accurate. Over forty serious business investors attended and requested the Celtus Business Plan which was only available on the day. Additionally, progress on potential City funding was being monitored closely by many others, as it was an innovative management approach, specifically for a potentially lucrative niche market. Lindy remembers it vividly

It was very nerve-racking. Our future hung in the balance. This was 14 years of our life's work and my husband's career, as well as my own. All the family would be affected. The boys had an impressive 140 song title releases registered with PRS, but it was a sinking ship. What would the boys be able to do? My 10 minute presentation speech had to have impact to try and convince these money-men. John spent three weekends rehearsing my diction in the studio and we played it back endlessly to get the inflections and pauses right. By then I was worn out and stressed to the max. There were a lot of frustrated tears. If this didn't work, nothing would.

Her carefully structured pitch, and the three song performance, went very well indeed. At the end, investors swarmed around them and enthusiastically promised to research the idea to the full then report back with a solid business offer. Specialized reports eventually flowed in, some of which were encouraging others, less so. The music was never an issue, but with this plan the main problem lay in the fact there was no 'Exit Strategy' ie no measure on when initial investments could be returned with estimated growth statistics for a 3-5 year period. As the press was full of music piracy stories and of crippling corporate losses, it seemed that backing a music project of this nature was akin to backing a horse. One report coldly stated

> These expectations are out of whack with reality. It's a *privilege* to be a musician and earn a living making music in this climate. But, they are not *entitled* to make a good living making music. Why should we fund mortgages? Scratch their own itch -get a day job like other wannabes. What you command is based on your commercial value.

Other media consultants stated the blindingly obvious saying 'The simplest, best marketing is an excellent infectious track that grabs you instantly and that you want to hear again. An audience only needs to hear it once, and 'get it' then it spreads far and wide. ' But that had been tried and, with the exception of a stab at the Eurovision Song contest (which was mentioned but never seriously considered), had failed. From a business perspective, it was the end of the road.

Celtus' final festival came at the Finsbury Park Fleadh, ironically on the same day as The Corrs (though on a different stage). The band was as dynamic as ever and despite all the gloom that lingered there was no shortage of smiles and enthusiasm emanating from the stage out over the crowd. John's low whistle on *The Awakening* (Pat and Sallie's wedding song) caressed thousands of punters enjoying the sunny day and was described by one reviewer as 'weaving a strong thread of magic.' Then, changing the tempo, that same crowd was led on a romp through versions of *Claddagh*, *Purple Diadem* and *Portrait*, where the interaction of the fiddle and whistle was as infectious and compelling as ever. Few present could have known, or believed, that they were watching a band whose career was over. The brothers, on the other hand, were well aware of what was going on and Pat had taken to the stage thinking

> This is it. This is the last festival and so lets go out with a smile on our faces. We knew when we were up on that stage that it was no more. We were packing up and heading for home. We had already asked people to look around for properties in Fermanagh.

The perfect swan song for Celtus to bow out on was a performance with the BBC Symphony Orchestra at Maida Vale Studios on 'Friday Night is Music Night' hosted by Angela Rippon. This was a black tie affair with a seated audience which went out live to a worldwide radio audience of 500,000 listeners. Lindy recalls 'It was terribly British and very old school' while John remembers feeling more than a bit out of place. Despite having played to colossal crowds all over the world for two decades it was now he who got the jitters

> I cannot tell you how much we were cacking ourselves that night. It was something we had never done before plus the fact it was the most intimidating thing we had ever, ever, ever done. We were on this stage alone, with all of the BBC concert orchestra sitting looking at us. All these guys read music and are all trained and we don't, we just pick it all up by ear. You don't feel too confident. And it is live.

Pat was the same, calling it

> The scariest thing I have ever done. There were classical violin players there who were absolutely amazing and there is me with my little Irish fiddle ... and I'm thinking 'I don't need this' and they are all looking as if to say 'We'll go on then, let's hear it.' I couldn't keep the bow still. I couldn't get away quick enough. I was intimidated. It was awful. The top violin players from the London Symphony Orchestra, and I've the neck of me to stand up and play my fiddle. I couldn't keep the bow straight I was so full of nerves.

Keyboard player, Dan Axtell, whose father was a classically trained pianist and who had studied Jazz thoroughly, shared no such concerns saying 'I grew up listening to orchestras rehearse and I'm up on my theory so it didn't really cross my mind.' In any case it passed off perfectly and Angela Rippon herself became an immediate convert. Years later she reflected on the nature of that 'compelling' quality

I just love the songs. The lyrics are wonderful, the way they use their voices, the combination of instruments, are all brilliantly arranged. The musicianship is incredibly engaging to listen to, ethereal, without ever being unfaithful to its roots.

But there was no getting away from the fact that this was Celtus' final performance and despite the enthusiasm of those around them, and the continued critical acclaim that such performances inevitably attracted, the journey was over. Lindy remembers

It was incredibly sad. Julian Spear (plugger), the boys and I knew it was the final show after five years. They played two songs and the last one was *Departure*. In muted moods we filed back to the bandroom -and seconds later an enthusiastic Angela Rippon came in personally to say how impressed she was and asked me to send her an album.

It was too little too late.

Shortly after the demise of Celtus it was reported in the music press that Muff had retired and that Sony S2 was no more. Peter Reichardt then appeared on the cover of *Music Week* departing EMI after ten consecutive and very successful years at the top, and soon Paul Burger was replaced as the Chairman of Sony. Cutbacks, it seems, had hit everyone.

Pat, Sallie and their daughter Shannon, were finished in England and the music industry in general, and were now lured by the relative security and simplicity of Fermanagh after such a long absence.

There was no way we were going to be able to continue as there were no finances. There is no point in flogging a dead horse. If there is no money how are you going to survive? You have to wake up and smell the coffee at some stage or other. We knew it had come to the end of the road. Anyway, the music industry was changing, trends were changing, the big Irish wave had been and gone and at some point you have to look and say 'That's it.'

John said 'It was one of those things where you all know it is at the end but you just don't bother saying it either. Pat headed in one direction and I headed off in another.' Without saying anything therefore, without fanfare or sentimental farewells, Pat and John had arrived at the end of a very long road. From Pulse, through Mama's Boys and then Celtus, they had circumnavigated the globe, seen the trials and tribulations of a business for which they had little taste, sold hundreds of thousands of albums and performed to literally millions of people. For the first time now they had no plans to continue their intertwined lives or even to make music together again.

Postscript

Having had one 'Woody Allen moment' too many ('whereby he wakes up and thinks he's got a brain tumor and says "What they hell are we going to do?" and then goes back to sleep forgetting all about it') Pat's family was glad to get back to Fermanagh. The decision had, in the end, been quite an easy one to make. Though they had no idea what they were going to do when they got to Northern Ireland they had run out of realistic options everywhere else. Pat thinks back on it

> So we packed up and tootled home to Ireland stopping off for a holiday in Wales on the way. Our whole world was in that car. 'Welcome to our world, it is in the boot of that car over there.' We laughed about it. We had to.

The local press was quick to jump on the news that one of Fermanagh's most famous musicians had come home and, accordingly, the *Sunday World* welcomed them all back to 'Life in the Slow Lane.' In return Pat told them that he had no regrets about the last two decades and no regrets either about letting the cycle come full circle back to Fermanagh. He summed it up saying 'We were just in it for the fun. I don't regret a moment. We were so lucky to have done what we did. It was a privilege.' The *Fermanagh Herald* printed an article called 'Mama's Boy comes home to Teemore' in which Pat drove the point home even further

> I've always loved it around here. It really has a strong place in my heart. I know it is a romantic notion but I'd always imagined it would be just the same as when I was a kid. I have noticed some changes but then it has been a long journey back.

The story of Mama's Boys and Celtus now belonged to the past. It was time to dwell not on that but on what lay ahead. Yes, there had been missed opportunities and certainly they had come very close to colossal success with two different bands, but that was over. At this stage in life, nothing mattered more than offering the family a stable home, getting back out and playing for the love of it, and teaching the next generation of up-and-coming violinists and guitarists. In keeping with the McManus family tradition Pat found 'I was surprised that a lot of people remembered me from the trad days and I took a lot of pleasure from passing on the tunes.' The purchase of a Ford van

Pat and Sallie back in Fermanagh: 'Life in the Slow Lane.'

John and Bobby Blotzer (Ratt) in 2009.

Pat and Warren de Martini (Ratt) in 2009.

and a PA, and teaming up with a couple of other decent musicians to work with, meant that Pat was back on the road before too long too. Today, with a small studio in his house and an accomplished manager in his wife, there are very few 'empty days' on the calendar both in Ireland and throughout Europe. Often he shares a stage with old colleagues and admirers such as Michael Schenker, Bernie Marsden, Wishbone Ash, Uriah Heep, the boys from Ratt, and long time hero, Johnny Fean of Horslips. There have been two CDs of new material too (*In My Own Time* and *2PM*) and a live DVD (*Live ... And In Time*), demonstrating that far from living on past glory Pat is moving on and going from strength to strength as a player and writer.

John still lives in London and continues to write and play with, amongst others, ex-Motörhead guitarist 'Fast' Eddie Clarke in Fastway. A DVD of them live in Tokyo a year or so ago suggests that he is still at his happiest when he is in front of a crowd. He has clearly lost little of his original enthusiasm when he says

> I can't express to you enough how much I have always been into heavy rock music. Maybe Tommy was into the more commercial stuff, and Pat was into experimenting, but I was strictly Black Sabbath, AC/DC, Judas Priest. I love being in a hard rock band, I love how it feels.

He has almost always got something on the go too in the form of film scores and TV compositions which to date include: *Someone in Particular, The Befriender, Birdman, The Grenada 17, Apparently, Rivers of Time, Welcome to Earth, Unload* & *Showclear*.

Looking back on it all, and far from agonizing over how they were done out of the acclaim that was rightfully theirs, both brothers display remarkably little regret. Much of the fault, they concede, was their own anyway and commercial success would just have pushed them further into the cut-throat world in which they were so clearly uncomfortable. Pat concludes

> Maybe I get disappointed for 5 minutes, then I forget all about it. I'm just happy when I am playing again. It never really left a scar on me I have to confess. We had a good time. And people say to us you didn't get this break or you didn't get that break, yes, but we also had the opportunities and we didn't take them either. It works both ways. If we had delivered a killer song we would have been in the stratosphere.

Philip Begley shares the same combination of pride, confusion and resignation, casting only a backward glance to conclude

Time passes and we all move on. I often think about Mama's Boys and especially Tommy and wonder if we had done this, or changed that, would it have made any difference. Still, we left behind a legacy in the field of Irish rock, something we can look back on and enjoy.

Lindy reminisces

Artists, labels and managers are all victims. Pat and John are, beyond any doubt, talented and great entertainers who have worked hard at that elusive hit song. The boys could play anything, but meandered in style and had intermittent gaps because of Tommy's illness and changing singers. As for labels, without a solution to the internet, they didn't see the transition and just ignored it. There is no subterfuge, just reality. You can't demand financial insurance. There is no recipe for success. That's just the way it is. Actually, 32 years to be venerated is a very long ride in the music business.

But perhaps it was Dante Bonutto who summed up an appreciation of longevity most succinctly when he said 'Mama's Boys' *raison d'etre* was the music, not the lifestyle. It will become the subject for connoisseurs in the future. These are musicians.' It was that simple.

A casual observer, had they walked into Robinson's pub in Belfast in early 2009, might have witnessed two middle-aged men chatting in the corner and laughing over a pint or two. On closer inspection any classic rock fan, having done a double-take, would have realized that Warren de Martini, the legendary Ratt guitarist, was one of them and Pat McManus the other. The razzamatazz of the rock circus may well have pulled out of town at the end of the 1980s, but for these two masters of their craft, these purist musicians, it matters little as they had always been in it for the long-haul. The American remembers

We shared the stage again with Pat's band last year in Belfast. I was so glad to see Pat I think I went on stage during his set and hugged him: a quarter of a century later – whoa! We met up in the in the old Scotch colored wood pub after the show. It was 'after hours' – lights out for five minutes then on again -a few pints and swapping stories.

Dave Ling rounds the story off with just a tantalizing trace of hope when he reminisces 'Mama's Boys gave me lots and lots of great memories. If Pat and John could get over the absence of Tommy (RIP), it would be thrilling to see them play once again, just for enjoyment's sake.'

The rest of the McManus family is still going strong too. Big John and Valerie have recently collaborated on a book and CD called *Hidden Fermanagh* which recorded for posterity, as John Gunn had done, the hidden musical gems from the Derrylin and Derrygonnelly regions of the county. They are proud of the achievements of their boys and share in reminiscing about them. Though the giant crowds at Reading, the euphoria of playing with Deep Purple at Knebworth, the excitement of travelling throughout the US with Twisted Sister, Ratt and Bon Jovi, the honor of playing the Albert Hall, and a thousand other Kodak moments are just memories now, beside the lake in Fermanagh the music goes on.

Beside the lake in Fermanagh the music goes on.

Afterword

At the time of putting the finishing touches to this book, Pat McManus, Paul McCanny, and I have just returned from a pub gig in Ardee where there wasn't even a stage. In a scene which Pete McCarthy would have adored, a stack of gear was set up in one corner with no great fuss, a few chords thrashed out to check that everything was still in tune, then followed by a blistering performance by the Pat McManus Band until the early hours of the morning. Though Pat still plays the stadiums, and takes to international stages watched by admiring crowds and critics alike, this, in Ardee, we all agreed on the drive home, is real live music ... the way music is meant to be. No entrance fee, a bar open until 2. 00am, a bunged lounge, and a crowd which included an old man waltzing with his wife, a purple haired punk pogo-ing, and a youth replicating every note on an air guitar. Tomorrow night it will happen again somewhere else. Getting into the van on a deserted Ardee Main Street at 3. 30 am, and starting back towards Fermanagh, Pat turned to me and said 'That was great craic, wasn't it?' I couldn't have agreed more. In the back of my mind though, I was just glad not to be walking home this time.

Appendices

Below, from left to right: John, the author, Davey. On the night of the walk home from Omagh (1983).

(Above) Tommy and the author just before setting off.

Pat and the author on the same night.

Sweet Cheater backstage in Derrygonnelly (1986).

Discography:

For a comprehensive discography, full track listings, DVDs, singles and compilation albums, see http://www. patmcmanus. co. uk/mamas. htm#

Albums: Mama's Boys

Official Bootleg -(c) Pussy 1980/re-issue 1981
Plug it in -(c) Pussy 1982/Ultra Noise 1982/Victor 1983/Albion 1986/ Castle 1986/Albion 1988
Turn it up -(c) Pussy 1983/Spartan 1983
Mama's Boys -(c) Pussy 1984/Jive 1984/Virgin 1984/Arista 1984
Power and Passion -(c) Jive 1985/Arista 1985/Bertelsman 1985/Gott 2006
Growing Up The Hard Way -(c) Jive 1987
Live Tonite (c) CTM Records 1990/Music For Nations 1991
Relativity -(c) CTM Records 1992/Angel Air 2001
The Collection -(c) Connoisseur VSOP 2000

Albums: CELTUS

Moonchild -(c) Sony S2 1997/Strathan Music 2005
Portrait -(c) Sony S2 1999
Rooted -(c) Music House International/Shamrock Music 2000
Live 2000 -(c) Shamrock Music/Evangeline Recorded Works 2001
What Goes Around -(c) Shamrock Music/Evangeline Recorded Works 2001

Index